THE AZTEC

Also by the same author

THE AZTEC
INDIANS OF MEXICO

SONIA BLEEKER

ILLUSTRATED BY
KISA SASAKI

WILLIAM MORROW & CO.
NEW YORK • 1963

Eighth Printing, September 1969

Copyright © 1963 by Sonia Bleeker
All rights reserved.
Published simultaneously in the Dominion of
Canada by George J. McLeod Limited, Toronto.
Printed in the United States of America.
Library of Congress Catalog Card Number 63-7198

Grateful recognition is given to Dr. Eric R. Wolf of the University of Michigan for reading and criticizing the manuscript.

CONTENTS

UNDERSTANDING THE AZTEC

THE glorious story of the Aztec Empire began, according to their own records, in 1168 and ended with the Spanish Conquest in 1520. The story of the Aztecan Indians continues in Mexico today. The remains of their temples, stonework, weaving, pottery, gold, silver, and feather work are still there for us to marvel at and admire.

But this ancient people is harder to understand than any other Indian civilization. At all times we should try to realize that their way of life sprang from a very deep sense of religious debt. The Aztec believed themselves to be a chosen people. They believed their creator, Quetzalcoatl (Kayt-zal'-ko-a'-tl), and their many other gods expected men to pay the debt for having been created and chosen by sacrificing human beings to them. The gods married, had children, and fought among themselves. Their favorite food and drink were human hearts and blood. This sacrificing of human beings is especially hard for us to understand and tolerate, because we believe that all life must be preserved.

There were, in the twelfth and thirteenth centuries, about a million Indians in what is now the United States and Canada, but there may have been some eight to sixteen million people to the south. The ancestors of these people may have come to the New World between 20,000 and 25,000 years ago—as all the other Indians came—across the Bering Strait from Asia. They wandered for thousands of years, settling here and there along the arctic coast, then traveling south along the Pacific, and eastward. Some settled in the eastern part of what is now the United States, some in the Midwest. As the population increased, groups moved south into Central America and from there to South America, until they filled the land and reached its end at Tierra del Fuego.

The migrants spread slowly, since they traveled on foot. They carried little food with them and depended on hunting along the way. The men and boys were constantly on the lookout for a rabbit or a deer, an armadillo, opossum, or bear. In northern Mexico there were also dangerous jaguars in the forests and, in the fields, ocelots or tigers, the gray or tawny relatives of the jaguar. Snakes had to be avoided along the trail.

As the group wandered and found a good place, they stopped to rest. If they knew about farming and if it was early in the year, they might even decide to stay a while and plant a crop of corn. Groups often split, because some moved more slowly than others, because food became scarce, or because the group grew too big to hunt together. As a new group formed, they selected from among themselves a leader, an older hunter who had already proved on the trail that he was devoted to the group.

Such a group, having settled, tended to develop common peculiarities and ways. Their speech, because they heard no new words, tended to develop differently from the other wandering people. They soon began to speak in a special way or, as we say, in a special dialect. The women, copying each other's basket and pottery designs and weaving skills, developed styles peculiar to their group. The men might perfect arrows and war clubs among themselves, and so these weapons also became peculiar to them. When they met strangers, they immediately recognized these people as different, and so named them after the river or lake, mountain or forest where they lived. Although the members of a group merely thought of themselves as "people," they usually called themselves "The People" in their special dialect.

In their early beginnings the Aztec were a poor people, known then as Tenochca (Teh-noch'-ka). As wanderers from the Northwest, the Tenochca began to move into the Valley of Mexico around 1168. The language they spoke was called Nahuatl (Nah'-wha-tl). It was related to the speech of the Toltec Indians of Central Mexico and to

AZTEC LANDS

the Chichimec, who were also latecomers into the Valley of Mexico. Nahuatl is also related to the language of the Utes and Hopi in western North America.

The Tenochca found the Valley of Mexico very attractive after the drier and colder Northwest, and they saw that this, clearly, was the place for them to settle. Soon this preference received religious meaning in the form of a legend, in which every Aztec believed.

The legend told that in 1168 they found in a cave the newborn god, Huitzilopochtli (Weet-zeel-oh-potch'-tly). The new god became their principal god, the God of the Sun and the God of War. Huitzilopochtli advised the Tenochca to gather together all their twenty clans, or families, and start a migration south. He prophesied that they would find new homes and farm lands on a lake in a valley. There, perched on a cactus, an eagle would fight a serpent. This would be the place for them to settle. The Tenochca took their new god along to guide and advise them, and according to the legend they found the place exactly as prophesied. There in the lake were the cactus, the eagle, and the serpent. This was to be their home. The eagle and the serpent became their emblem, and are today Mexico's emblem.

The Valley of Mexico is between 7000 and 8000 feet above sea level. It is surrounded and protected by tall mountains. Even though its two tallest mountains, Popocatepetl, or Smoking Mountain, and Iztaccihuatl (Ees'-tak-see'-wa-tl), or White Lady, are over 17,000 feet high and snow-covered the year round, the temperature in the valley is mild. It is not too cold in winter, which is the dry part of the year, and not too hot in summer, which is the wet part of the year. At the time of the Tenochcan arrival the center of the valley was occupied by a large salt lake, Lake Texcoco (Tess-ko'-ko), which had several fresh-water streams flowing into it. The nearby lakes of Chapultepec and Xochimilco (So'-chee-meel'-ko) were bodies of fresh water that were also fed by streams.

The marshy shores of these lakes were filled with ducks and geese and birds of all kinds. The waters were filled with fish. The valley was green the year round. In the wet season vegetation became rich and thick. Even in dry weather there was always an abundance of flowers, which the Tenochca loved.

Other Indians had already peopled this rich valley. They were all farmers, who raised corn, beans, squash, peppers, tomatoes, sunflowers, and tobacco. The people of the Valley of Mexico had been living there for 5000 to 10,000 years and had developed fine arts and crafts in addition to farming. They had also built tall temples to their gods and had established ceremonies and rituals to honor them each year.

These farmers did not suspect or foresee that the Tenochcan wanderers whom they welcomed would one day become one of the greatest powers in the Americas, to be placed beside the civilizations of the Mayan Indians in the southeastern part of Central America and the Incan Indians of Peru. Nor did these valley people foresee that the Tenochca would become their masters for the next three centuries. All too often in history, kindness is not repaid with kindness.

But, in the beginning, the people of the valley were glad to let these humble Tenochca get un-

used and unwanted swampland around Chapultepec. On it the Tenochca built small huts of mud
and wattle and began to work the fertile soil. They
already knew how to farm and learned even more
from their neighbors. Surrounded by these hard-
working Indians, the Tenochca settled down con-
tentedly in the region of Chapultepec. For about
a century they farmed, wove clothing, and made
pottery and mats for their small homes, and baskets in which to store their harvests.

The years went by, and their population increased. More land was needed, so the Tenochcan
farmers scooped up dirt and mud from the shal-
low lake bottom and piled it against retaining
walls of reeds. These formed huge floating,
swampy islands, which they called chinampas.
The roots of the plants and shrubs they planted in
them spread and held the soil together. Before
each planting season the Tenochca scooped up
more of this fertile, marshy soil and spread a fresh
layer over the chinampas. People went back and
forth in their small canoes around them, tending
their crops and gardens and carrying the harvest
home and to market.

The Tenochca were a short, sturdy, brown-skinned people, with straight black hair and brown eyes. Their dress was very simple. A man wore a wide woven breechcloth and a mantle for warmth. The mantle was a square piece of cloth that reached to the knee and was knotted over one shoulder. In the marshes the farmers went barefoot, but they wore sandals when walking on the ground. The women wore a long wrap-around skirt and a huipil (wee-peel'), or blouse, with a square neck. They were usually barefoot. The clothing was woven on narrow looms, and the thread was either of pounded, coarse maguey fiber or cotton.

This basic dress remained the same throughout Aztecan times, but as they acquired wealth through conquest, crafts, and skills, the Tenoch-can women began to weave elaborate mantles for their men. These were of cotton but were finished with colorful bird feathers, gold thread, and ornaments, with wide, brilliant borders of geo-metric design. The ends of the simple breechcloths were also dyed and elaborately decorated with em-broidery. As a man grew wealthier and gained honors, the ends of his breechcloth tended to get longer and to carry more extravagant designs. In addition, men also began to wear another cloth around the middle, which served as a wide belt. Their simple sandals were now trimmed with fancy lacings of leather, sewed with silver and gold thread. Women's clothing, too, took on more color. The borders of their skirts and huipils were embellished with decorations.

The early Tenochca usually went bareheaded or wore a simple cloth band to hold their long hair in place. Later they wore jewelry, necklaces, arm bands, lip plugs, and earplugs. As the artists made new images of the gods, their clothing also became more elaborate. Men and women dressed up in their best finery for ceremonials to honor the gods. But the everyday dress of the Tenochca tended to be simple.

With prosperity and an ever-increasing population, the young Tenochcan men began to look for wives among the neighboring villages. They raided neighboring peoples and stole their women. This led to war. The neighbors—the Tepanec, the Culhua, and the Xochimilca—allied themselves against the Tenochca and defeated them. For a time some of the Tenochca became slaves. Others escaped to an island in Lake Texcoco.

The Tenochca watched for an opportunity to regain their freedom. This opportunity presented itself when the Culhua went to war with their neighbors, the Xochimilca (So'-chee-meel'-kah). The Tenochca fought on the side of the Culhua, and the Culhua defeated the Xochimilcans. Whereupon, the Culhuan chief, Coxcox (Cosh-cosh), gratefully offered his daughter to the Tenochcan chief in marriage. The chief took the girl, but instead of marrying her he offered her, in turn, to Toci, the earth goddess, as a sacrifice. Chief Coxcox was understandably upset when he came to attend his daughter's wedding ceremony and saw instead a priest dressed in her skin.

The Tenochca explained that Huitzilopochtli, their god of war and of the sun, did not want them to ally themselves with other people. He had destined them for war and wished them to avoid any alliances that might lead to peace and friendship with their neighbors. Because they were the Sun God's chosen people, the Tenochca had to obey. They were now committed to war with their neighbors, and Coxcox immediately went to war against them. The Tenochca fled and joined their clansmen on the islands in Lake Texcoco.

Here, in a place safe from invasion and attack, they started building temples to their gods. In 1325, according to Aztecan records, they founded in Lake Texcoco the city of Tenochtitlán, which eventually became the capital of the Aztec Empire. To the north of it, another city was founded and called Tlaltelolco. Tenochtitlán was soon crowded with temples, the rulers' palaces, and homes. The city of Tlaltelolco remained more spacious, with a magnificent pyramid temple to Huitzilopochtli and a vast market place.

At first these islands could be reached only by canoe, but as the population grew and the homes and temples on the islands increased in number, the Tenochca built causeways to connect their capital with the mainland. In time, there were three such causeways connecting these towns with the mainland. Also, two viaducts were built to supply the towns with fresh water.

The causeways were built up of soil and stone, but the Tenochcan engineers very cleverly left gaps in them and built bridges over the gaps. These enabled canoes to pass underneath and to circle the towns. In time of danger the bridges could be lifted, and the cities would be isolated and safe. In the early days the number of people in canoes going back and forth through the cities' canals were as numerous as those traveling on land.

As a warring nation, the Tenochca were invited into alliances with other neighboring peoples, the Texcocans and the Tlacopáns. They fought well.

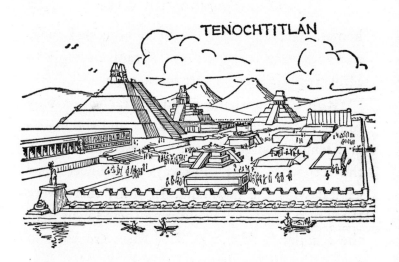

TENOCHTITLÁN

As a reward for their conquests, Tenochcan warriors acquired land on the mainland as gifts. The land was farmed for them by the conquered tribesmen. These Tenochca grew into a wealthy class, which formed a nobility, so that, in time, the Tenochca were made up of several classes. There were royal families, from which rulers were chosen. There were noblemen, who ran the government and led the wars. They became war captains, warriors, tribute collectors, and merchants. The lowest class of Tenochca was made up of craftsmen and farmers. There were also Tenochcan slaves. The majority of them were war

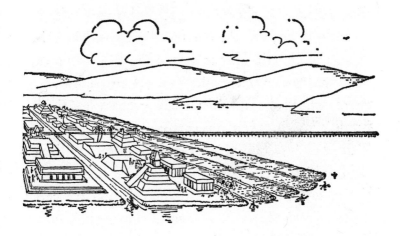

captives, but some were men and women who, in time of need due to crop failures or illness in the family, hired themselves out to work in a nobleman's household. The children of the Tenochcan slaves were free.

The Aztec dynasty began in 1376. The first ruler was called Acamapichtli. He was a neighboring Culhuan Indian. Because he was an able war chief, the Tenochca invited him to rule over them and lead them into war. This he did most successfully, and even fought his own people. Acamapichtli died in 1395 and was succeeded by a Tenochca, called Huitzilhuitl. In all there were nine rulers. Of these, Itzcoatl, who ruled from 1428 to 1440, was the one most interested in unifying the domain into an Aztec Empire. He even destroyed some of the old Tenochcan records, so there would be no historical witness to their humble origins. His reforms really launched the Tenochca into building an empire and a civilization, which recognized and used the best of all the conquered peoples. This civilization we call Aztec. In time, too, the Tenochcan people, now mixed through marriage with their neighbors, began to be called Aztecans.

As the Aztec Empire spread, reaching out east and west through Central Mexico and south into western Guatemala, the number of their gods grew. The Aztecans adopted the gods of conquered people to add to their own religious strength. With such a great number of gods, the people to be sacrificed to feed them increased, too. It is reported that the Aztecan ruler Ahuitzotl sacrificed 20,000 captives and that Montezuma II sacrificed 12,000 enemy warriors at one time. These were Zapotecan warriors of Oaxaca (Waha'-kah), whom the Aztec conquered.

Montezuma II (1503–1520) was the last ruler under the Aztec Empire. Each of these rulers had aimed at enlarging the Aztec lands. Before the coming of the Spanish, most of Mexico—some 371 towns—paid tribute to the Aztec. The Aztecans did not attempt to govern every part of their domain. They let the conquered people keep their own governments. But they sent in administrators and tribute collectors, who helped enforce the collection of tribute and drafted warriors for the Aztecan army. The Aztecan rulers were always ready to send their army to war. If victorious, they would have more captives to sacrifice—to pay their debt to the gods for such prosperity and success.

The rich tribute made the palaces of the rulers show places of all that was finest in their civilization. Their storehouses bulged with goods. The rulers showered their own warriors and nobles with gifts.

Yet all was not completely harmonious, even among the Aztecan nobility and royalty. From time to time a noble or a soothsayer dared to speak out against human sacrifice and bloodshed. A few men dared question the cruel will of the gods. Legends grew among the people that Quetzalcoatl the Wise, who created mankind, had departed from Mexico, because he objected to war and to human sacrifice. He had left for the East, they said, across the ocean. It was predicted that with Montezuma II the Aztec Empire would come to an end. Quetzalcoatl would return and become head of the realm—to rule without war and without human sacrifice.

2

VILLAGE LIFE

Six hundred years ago in Aztecan times, as in Mexico today, small villages crowded together overlooking their cornfields, their cotton fields, and their neat rows of maguey. When the sun set and dark engulfed the land, the huts on the hillsides were each lit suddenly, as if by magic, by a single small light—a burning torch of the pitch-soaked, fragrant ocote pine. The yellow rays glimmered through the chinks in the wattled walls of the huts. The landscape was no longer lonely and dark. Filled with dozens of wavering, beckoning, friendly little yellow rays, it must have been a welcome sight indeed to the lonely Tenochcan merchants and their carriers, when they traveled at night to save time, moving slowly on foot under their heavy burdens.

Inside an Aztecan household there was little furniture. People sat on mats on the earthen floor. They slept on mats, too, which they rolled out for the night, and covered themselves with a mantle. In a corner of the room was a small fire pit, encircled with stones. Here the mother of the household prepared the two daily meals for her family —one early in the morning before the men went off to work in the cornfields and the other when they returned home. Over a few stones she balanced a large griddle, a *comalli* (ko-mah'-yee). The *comalli* was heated by a small fire underneath. On it she tossed thin corn pancakes, called tortillas (tore-tee'-yas). This was the staple for all meals and feasts, as bread is with us. In the old days the Aztec made very large tortillas, the size of a dinner plate.

After soaking the starchy, soft corn kernels in

water overnight, the mother crushed them with a handstone on a large flat stone called a metate. She mixed the ground corn with water to form dough. With the help of her daughter or an old woman, she then slapped and flattened balls of this dough into tortillas between the palms of her hands and tossed them onto the griddle for a quick roasting on both sides.

The father and boys ate together, dipping the hot tortillas in a pepper sauce or a sauce of ground beans. Meat they seldom ate, because game was already scarce in Mexico even in Aztecan times. Housewives fattened turkeys and small dogs for festive occasions, and there were ducks, quail, and small birds, which the men and boys shot as a treat for the family meal. They had no chickens then.

After the men had finished their meal, the women ate and then carefully wrapped up any leftover tortillas in a piece of cloth, so a hungry child might have a snack during the day. From morning to sunset was a long time for a youngster to wait for a regular meal. A baby was nursed at any time it cried for food, and it was not weaned for about three years. The change to only two meals a day was too great for small children, so they, too, ate when hungry.

After each meal household matters were discussed, and the children were instructed about behavior and customs. The parents spoke of what was proper and what was wrong behavior. Children learned how to sit correctly. A young man usually sat cross-legged on a mat. A young girl always tucked her feet modestly under her long skirt. Children learned at an early age how to speak to their parents, to relatives, and to strangers. By the time a child reached his eighth year, he knew proper behavior, and there was no excuse for doing otherwise. However, if boys or girls persisted in acting differently from what they knew was customary, their parents were shamed.

The Tenochca treated their children with kindness and affection. But if a child of eight misbehaved, the parents punished him. A parent took the child's hand and pricked it with a maguey thorn. When a child misbehaved it not only offended its parents and relatives, but also the gods. It was the religious custom to prick the tongue, cheeks, ears, and hands at the temple as an offering to the gods and to court their favor.

The kindness and patience in the home extended to the village, too. Children were surrounded by the familiar faces of older people, who tried to guide them. A Tenochca grew up surrounded by his clansmen—his relatives.

The Tenochca believed that their original twenty clans had long ago descended from a common ancestor. Each clan was made up of many related families. Each clan member, because of this blood relationship, was obligated to treat every other clan member with the greatest consideration. The loyalty of clan members covered every phase of village life, and they were always ready to help one another. Clan members preferred to live close together in the same village, and they worked together in the cornfields, which belonged to the clan as a whole. Their sons played together and went to school together. After marriage, a young woman was obligated to her husband and his family. She seldom visited her own people, and her children belonged to their father's clan. The sons stayed on in the same village and farmed the pieces of land that the village council gave them. Their clansmen helped them build their houses when they married. The oldest son inherited his father's house and possessions and became head of the family.

A birth was not announced until the village priest studied the religious books and calendar to make sure that the birthday was a lucky day. The Aztec compiled a very impressive calendar of sacred events and ceremonies. It was most important for a child's successful future that its birthday be a day recommended as lucky in the calendar. If the actual date of birth was not considered lucky by the priest, he merely switched the birthday to another luckier date and announced that the child had been born on that day. Four days after this recognized date of birth, the child's father called the grandparents and some clansmen together for a feast and a naming ceremony. A priest also attended. If the village was very small the village chief acted as priest.

The women of the clan helped the mother clean house and spread out fresh mats. They gathered flowers and greens for decorations. The guests came wearing their best mantles and all their jewelry. Among the simple village folk the jewelry usually consisted of some shell ornaments, plaited bracelets, or arm bands of feathers. Each guest inspected the baby. If it was a boy, the happy father held his infant's tiny hands, in which had been placed a toy club and bow and arrows and a tiny digging stick. Because of their belief in magic, the Aztec thought this would make the boy grow up to be a good farmer and a brave warrior. If it was a girl, the mother held up the infant's hands, clutching a toy spindle, a little cooking pot, and a toy metate for crushing corn, so the baby would grow up to be a good housekeeper and wife.

The name for the child had already been decided by the priest with the parents' consent. Usually a boy bore the name of the day on which he was born, or he might be named for a famous warrior ancestor or some favored animal. A girl usually bore the name of a flower.

We are fortunate to know these fine details from the family life of the Tenochca through eyewitnesses. These intimate details were written down over four hundred and fifty years ago by a few men who came with the Spanish conquerors and lived in Mexico with the Aztec Indians. Among these men was a Franciscan friar-missionary, Bernardino de Sahagún. Friar Sahagún lived between 1490 and 1590. In order to convert the Indians to Christianity, he learned Nahuatl and was able to speak freely with his converts, as well as with various noblemen who became his friends. We owe much to him and to the books he wrote, entitled *A General History of the Things of New Spain*.

From Sahagún we learn the very touching speech a Tenochcan grandparent made during a birthday ceremony. As he fondled the infant, the grandparent said, "O my beloved grandson. You have been loaned to us by our gods for a short time only. You have endured great suffering and fatigue to come here. You come here to the earth to suffer. This is a place of bitterness. Beloved grandson, you are the image of our ancestors."

The grandfather then turned to the infant's mother and said, "O my beloved daughter, you have endured great suffering and fatigue. You have separated from your beloved child, the precious feather and jewel that the Lord has sent us. We shall love him as a precious necklace, as a precious stone bracelet. Do not let any accidents befall you or the child. Be calm and modest. Take care of your child. Even in your sleep, with the child beside you, be careful of him. Never leave him unwatched, for he has been given to us by God."

Sahagún was not without a sense of humor, too. He then described the behavior of the guests, who were seating themselves to partake of the birthday feast. "The guests rushed about like fools, hurrying, hastening to grab the garlands of flowers prepared for them. Each wanted to be recognized by everyone. Each wanted to be seen, to hear his name spoken."

After seating themselves on the mats set out for them, the guests began the simple feast. But first they threw into the fire bits of the tortillas and filling they had been served, to share the food with the gods. They also poured a few drops of their drinks over the fire. At that time the Aztec favored a drink called *octli*, which is still popular in Mexico today and is called pulque (pool'-kay). Pulque is the fermented sap of the maguey plant. Sap of the maguey is sucked out from the center of the plant by means of a long tube or gourd. The opening is then carefully sealed, so the plant does not suffer. The sap is placed in a large earthen jar and permitted to ferment into a kind of beer. Women and children, however, drank pinole (pee-no'-lay), which was a nourishing mixture of ground corn meal and water. At the end of the meal, if the family could afford it, they also served a dessert of *chocólatl*—chocolate sweetened with honey and flavored with cinnamon.

After the meal the guests sat talking, making witty remarks, and laughing, according to Sahagún, "as though their sides would split." Some began to sing. The songs were usually sad, perhaps like the songs full of tears that the Mexican people favor today. There was no unity in the singing. Each person sang to please himself and the gods. Some people hummed tunes and chants. Others raised their voices in their own favorite songs. Each tried to outdo his neighbor, and all sang at the same time.

The birthday feast ended late at night, and the guests departed for their homes. Some of the old clansmen, who were permitted by custom to drink all the pulque they desired, had already fallen asleep on the mats where they sat, and no one disturbed them.

Between the ages of three and eight a boy was his father's responsibility. Patiently and kindly, the father watched his son and taught him year after year all the skills he knew in farming, hunting, and in making his simple tools and weapons. Daily, from about the age of six, a boy accompanied his father to the fields. After the corn had been planted with a very simple digging stick, they worked with a hoe all day, day after day, to keep the weeds out, to heel the young corn plants, and to watch over the shoots of beans, chili or peppers, and gourds. These were planted between the rows of bushy cornstalks. Even a small boy could help in this weeding. He could also shoo away birds that were after the young, milky corn kernels.

Girls stayed with their mother until marriage. There were some exceptions to this. Some girls might be dedicated at the age of ten to a special school at the temple. There they received special training in fine weaving, pottery, caring for the temple, and preparing meals for the priests. At home a girl watched and learned from her mother all the household skills. She learned to make different kinds of thread, to weave cloth, to mend and sew, and to make mats, pots, and griddles. She also learned to cook, to make tortillas and chili sauces. Like father and young son, mother and daughter were inseparable. They became more devoted to each other through the bonds of common experience in facing the continuous work of the household, in making economies so the food would stretch from one harvest to the next, and in splurging when there was a feast. The dignity of a man's home demanded that there be no limit to hospitality. A man's worth was judged not by the amount of food he had stored away after the harvest, but by the amount he gave to the needy each year.

At fourteen or fifteen the son of a farmer was sent to the village school. The teachers were old men and warriors, usually members of the same clan as their students. They knew the youths well, and the youths knew and respected them. The boys lived in the school for four or five years, learning Aztecan customs, history and legends, arts and crafts. They also trained for war. The old warriors drilled the boys for battle and taught them to use spears and bows and arrows. They taught them to use the atlatl, which was very important in war. This was a narrow wooden throwing board, with a hook at one end. The thrower held the atlatl in one hand and balanced his spear on top of it, hooking it at the end. With his right hand holding the atlatl, he swung it forward, hurtling the spear on its way. With the atlatl he could throw his spear farther and with more force.

Boys also learned to use shields. The boy warriors carried them on the left arm and used them to parry enemy spears and arrows. The small shield, made of interlaced reeds and wood and covered with hide, could be manipulated rapidly and was very effective in saving a warrior's life.

The crafts the boys learned were those of future stonecutters, wood carvers, painters, sculptors, and goldsmiths. Whenever a boy showed a particular aptitude for an art or craft, he was singled out to be sent to a school connected with a temple for further training. Such a boy eventually devoted his entire time to his craft, and he no longer farmed. The royal family or the nobleman for whom he would work in town supplied him and his family with food and with cotton and leather for weaving cloth and making sandals.

The boys also listened to daily talks by the old men about their duties to the people in the village and, above all, their debts to the gods. All festivals must be strictly observed if the Tenochca were to keep their might.

At twenty a boy was ready for marriage. His schooling was finished. A girl was ready for marriage at fifteen or sixteen. Usually the parents first consulted with the chief or priest of the village as to whether their son's choice of a wife would form a lucky union. The priest checked on the birth dates of the couple. If the two dates together were deemed lucky, he approved the marriage. If he found them unlucky, the parents urged their son to select another girl. A couple usually married because each agreed to the marriage. When the right girl was selected, the boy's parents sent two clanswomen to the girl's family with gifts. These were small gifts. The larger ones from the boy's parents would come later, when the girl's family had agreed to the marriage and to losing a daughter. In turn, the girl's parents gave the bride a dowry of cloth, mats, foods, and pottery, with which to start her housekeeping.

After several visits from the clanswomen, the parents finally agreed to the marriage and a day was set at once for the simple wedding ceremony. The ceremony took place in the new house of the bridegroom, which his clansmen had helped build. A clanswoman lifted the bride over the threshold of her new home and seated her next to the bridegroom. The edge of the mantle the bride wore was tied to the bridegroom's mantle as they sat in front of the old men and women who came to talk to them. Each old clansman took his turn in advising the young couple on ways to behave toward each other, proper ways to honor the gods, and ways to work for the welfare of their clan.

After the marriage ceremony the young couple

was parted for four days. Under the supervision
of their elders, they fasted and prayed. On the
fifth day the young bride started on her housekeeping and baked the first tortillas for her husband. The husband went to the fields and began
work on the piece of land that the clan chiefs had
allotted to him.

If the young husband was fortunate, he might
live happily with his wife for a year or two without being called to war. They would have a child,
and the young father would begin to feel he was
an important member of the clan. Soon older men
would invite him to the clan's councils. They
would ask him to act as messenger at first and to
do some menial jobs for the council. Later, if he
worked hard and prospered, he might begin to
speak at the councils and have the older people
listen to him. As their respect for him grew, the
young man would be asked to be responsible for a
feast in honor of a village god. He might also be
asked to sit as judge and settle quarrels among the
villagers and set punishments for misbehavior. In
all these village activities a man did not stint
either of his time or of his food. Through his

generosity a man gained appreciation. Through fearlessness in war he gained respect and the chance of rising to the highest office, that of chief or priest, in the clan and village.

The clans governed themselves by electing one official as secretary-treasurer, to keep records for the clan on field allotments, marriages and births, and taxes for the rulers. Another was elected to act as sheriff, to preserve order. When the call to war came, the sheriff acted as war chief and was responsible to the government for drafting warriors. He also commanded his clan members in battle. Each clan elected one man as speaker for the supreme council. Only the oldest and wisest men attained this important post.

In turn, the supreme council, which represented all twenty clans, selected four officials to control the army. The twenty clans were divided into four brotherhoods, or phratries. Each of the selected four officials was in charge of one such phratry. One of these four men selected by the council became the ruler of the land.

It was not likely, as time went on, that a farm boy would rise to this supreme position. The children of noblemen had the better chance because of their better education and training. A farm boy who proved himself especially brave in war and in bringing back a large number of captives might gain the great honor of becoming an Eagle or Tiger Warrior and command a unit of men. Such honor assured him gifts of land and jewels from the rulers after a war and also an entrance into heaven, where he would become a companion of the Sun God.

Only when he reached the ripe age of fifty-two was a man freed of obligation to the clan and the village and of taxes to the government. But in a society where wars occured so frequently, not many men reached the age of fifty-two. For a woman of fifty-two the housework continued. She still had her daily cooking to do, she still had to grind all the corn for the tortillas, and she always had to weave cloth and help care for her grand-children.

3

LIFE IN THE CITY

TENOCHCAN noblemen were also members of a clan. Their families had grown away from the soil, and they had slaves to work the fields for them. They no longer lived near their lands, but settled in towns. Their houses were more solidly built than farmers' homes. The stonemasons used rubble, stone, and plaster, colored red or white. The buildings had flat roofs, and each had one or two rooms, one behind the other. The doors usually faced a bright patio, which was like a garden. As the nobleman's family grew, he added more buildings. All surrounded the patio. In Tenochtitlán houses were raised on a stone foundation to keep them dry. Another story might be added to the flat roof, with an outside stairway leading up to it.

Some noblemen had more than one wife. Each wife had her own house, where she supervised the cooking done by female slaves and cared for her children. The slaves did the weaving, although noblewomen who were skilled weavers liked to sit at their own looms.

The nobility celebrated the birth of their children, the naming of them, and their marriages with the same customs as those of the common people, except that they usually had more visitors. The common people liked to be known and greeted at these ceremonies. Noblemen and noblewomen were even prouder. Sahagún tells that some of the noblemen were so touchy that if the servant who was assigned to call out the noblemen's names on arrival failed to greet a couple in the proper manner, or if the food was not served them properly, the couple's faces would turn red

and they would depart in anger. The next day the host had to give the offended guests a special feast, so that they would not wish him or his child ill luck.

Men dressed in colorful, sumptuously embroidered breechcloths, mantles, and sandals. The women wore elaborate skirts and huipils. All wore jewels, gold and silver necklaces, chest ornaments, earplugs, and lip plugs. Men and women wore elaborately knitted stockings with their leather sandals. The men's headdresses were ornate, with tall feathers and stone inlays. The women wore their hair in two long braids, in which gold and silver threads were interlaced. Men and women wore shiny headbands and arm bands of gold and feathers.

From childhood, a nobleman never worked with his hands. While a six-year-old commoner worked beside his father in the cornfield, a six-year-old nobleman spent his day playing games. Young slaves watched over him and played with him.

The social obligations of a nobleman began early, however. He had to show respect for old people. When a child saw an old person, he stopped his playing and spoke to him. Sahagún quotes an example of a nobleman's son, who called out to an old man, "Come here, beloved grandfather, that I may bow to you." And the old man, touched by the young nobleman's courtesy, readily replied, "O my beloved grandson. You have indeed favored me, little jewel, precious feather. May all go well with you."

At the age of twelve or thirteen a young nobleman's parents had the choice of sending him to either one of two schools. The first was the Telpochcalli, the House of Youth, which was similar to the schools for the children of the commoners. Here the youngsters were taken in hand by warriors to learn the arts of war and to gain skills. But a good part of the time was also spent in religious education, in fasting, and in prayers. The young people pierced their tongues and ear lobes as acts of penance.

Wise men and priests came to teach them the history of the Aztec, their sacred calendars, and how to keep records of collected tribute. They learned the geography of their lands, the location of towns that were paying tribute to the Aztec, the names of their chiefs, and the products of each conquered region. This they would have to know when they grew up and were appointed as tribute collectors or administrators.

The second school was called the Cálmecac, which means Row of Houses, and there the boys studied to be priests. Most of the noblemen in Tenochtitlán sent their children to the Cálmecac. Common children also attended this school. Sometimes a commoner decided, on the birth of a son, to dedicate him to the priesthood. A priest would then take the infant to the temple for his birthday and naming ceremony. The priest painted the child's face black and hung a string of holy wooden beads on his neck. The child's soul was thus transferred to the beads. These beads were left at the temple when the child was returned to his parents. This meant that his soul belonged to the temple. When the child was old enough to enter the Cálmecac his parents brought him to the temple to begin his education as a priest.

Life for the youngsters at the Cálmecac was

rigorous, the discipline severe. These noblemen's children were being trained for a life of fasting, penance, and self-denial as Aztec warrior-priests. All slept on the cold, hard floors of the school. Often the boys had to get up in the middle of the night, plunge into a cold pool to purify themselves, and then attend sacrifices and prayers. The youngsters gathered wood and kept the temple fires going. They also carried water for the temple. They swept and decorated it with flowers. To do penance, boys soaked bundles of maguey leaves in their own blood. In the middle of the night, dressed only in breechcloths and shivering with pain and cold, they walked alone to a high spot near the temple to deposit their bundles of blood for the gods.

If a child broke a rule of the Cálmecac his parents were fined. Should they fail to pay the fine, a boy might be thrown into the water and beaten. For a major mistake a boy was simply expelled from the school.

The priests read to their pupils from their sacred books of guidance, the *tonalamatl*, and taught the future young priests to read. The *tonalamatl* were tall books. The paper in them was the pounded bark of the wild fig, or *amatl*, painted with a white clay. Each book consisted of a single folded sheet. The writing in them was in pictographs. By combining a picture of an animal with another animal or object, the reader formed syllables and words. History and events were recorded with such pictographs. Each god was recognized, because he was drawn in his characteristic costume. Dates were shown by a system of special signs and numbers.

The Aztec counted in twenties.

1 was a dot or a finger.

10 was ten dots or fingers; 15 was fifteen dots or fingers.

20 was a flag.

400, 20 times 20, had a sign meaning hairs, as in a feather.

410 was shown as a feather and ten dots.

450 was shown as a feather, two flags, and ten dots.

8000, 400 times 20, was shown as a bundle or bag.

With constant repetition, the *tonalamatl* in a temple became familiar to its students. When they needed to know a date or to check its importance

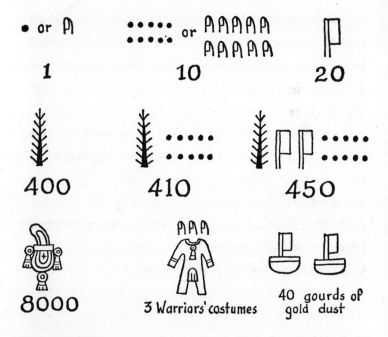

| | 1 | | 10 | | 20 |

1

10

20

400

410

450

8000

3 Warriors' costumes

40 gourds of gold dust

they knew from memory which *tonalamatl* to tackle for the needed information.

After a few years of study at the Cálmecac the young noblemen looked thin and worn. Their ear lobes, lips, and tongues had been pierced many times in prayer with the thorns of maguey. But they survived and were tougher than those who attended the Telpochcalli, even though they had not had as much practice with weapons of war.

At fifteen or sixteen the young noblemen of both schools were taken to war. The parents of a young man about to go to war put him in the care of a warrior. They gave the older man gifts and begged him to take care of their son. The only difference between the warriors trained at the Cálmecac and those of the Telpochcalli was that the young priests had a red semicircle painted from their temples to their chins. When an enemy met such a young warrior, he knew that he possessed sacred powers that watched over him, and that he would be harder to overcome.

War as the Aztecans fought it was grim, but it usually consisted of a single battle. If the Aztec won the battle they returned home with captives. If they lost, the survivors returned home without captives. All wars were primarily fought to get captives to sacrifice to the gods. Of course the booty of war, which the warriors brought back, added to the wealth of the rulers, as did the tribute they would collect henceforth from the conquered peoples.

The army was organized into small units of twenty men, which were under the command of the brave Eagle and Tiger Warriors. Such small units were often ordered on scout duty and raids. For battle these units combined into larger groups of 200 and 400 men. The chief of a clan was in command of each of these larger groups. Each large group was a member of one of the four phratries, under the command of one of the four supreme chiefs.

The Aztec, even in their heyday, preferred a short and quick war not too many days' travel from their capital. They preferred to get allies to fight a war for them rather than send their own men over long distances. Long marches exhausted the warriors. They marched to war on foot and had to return the same way. The wounded had to be carried by other warriors. They had no way to transport extra weapons, arrows, and spear points, except on the backs of the soldiers themselves and their few carriers. Women had to march with the army to prepare food, which they brought with them. The army was not allowed to ask for food along the route, and stealing from a cornfield was punishable by death. Only when in extreme hunger were the soldiers permitted to take a few ears of corn from a field. It was feared if they took food, it might antagonize an ally, through whose land they were passing. The ally might then turn against them and attack them from the rear.

There was no approaching a region by stealth and falling upon an enemy at dawn, as the Indians of North America used to do. An Aztecan army was seen and heard by the ever-watchful villagers long before it reached its destination. When the warriors finally met the armed enemy, they fell upon him with ferocious yells and shouts, brandishing war clubs and slings, hurtling spears with sharp, curved obsidian points from their atlatls, and letting loose a flood of arrows. After the arrows were exhausted and the spear points broken, the men threw themselves into hand-to-hand combat, protected by their trusty shields and padded cotton armor. The disarmed enemies became captives and were bound and led back to Tenochtitlán, their fate known to themselves as well as to their captors.

During the battle the seasoned warriors watched the behavior of the young warriors assigned to them. In many cases, where a young man showed bravery, the older warrior guided him and helped him to success by securing for him a captive whom he could lead back. Several men could capture one enemy and get credit for it.

The success of the Aztec in their wars was due largely to a new class of men and women that sprang up. This was the merchant class, or the pochteca, who traveled all over Mexico to trade and also to spy. Some of these merchants had humble beginnings. At first they were people who went to local markets to trade or exchange the surplus produce of some of their clansmen for the things they wanted. These merchants found they liked trading, and so set themselves up as pochteca. In time these pochteca grew in wealth and importance. They traveled all over Mexico, into Guatemala, Yucatán, and even Panama. Craftsmen in Tenochtitlán began to depend on them for materials, for certain dyes, and for the gold and jade used in making jewelry.

Merchants left Tenochtitlán on foot with a large number of loaded carriers. The men who were carriers could travel all day with a pack of sixty to one hundred pounds on their backs. They traded the products of Tenochtitlán, such as rolls of finely woven cloth, lumps of obsidian, and maguey rope. Before leaving, each merchant consulted with a priest to make sure the day was a lucky one for such a departure. A special god, Yacatecuhtli—the merchants' god—watched over these men. Merchants prayed to Yacatecuhtli and made sacrifices to him before and after each journey.

On the west coast the merchants traded for sea shells, feathers of tropical birds, and cacao, from which the Aztec made *chocólatl*, their favorite drink. From Oaxaca they brought gold and turquoise, also mantles of fine cloth, and breechcloths. From the Veracruz region came finely carved stones, jewelry, earplugs, lip plugs, nose plugs, rings, skins of wild animals, figurines and pottery, and capes with fine feather designs.

When merchants returned from a trading expedition, they were received with great honor by the Aztec ruler. The nobility met them at a causeway to Tenochtitlán and marched in double file with them to the palace. When the procession reached the palace, the servants lighted bowls of sacred copal incense in their honor. The Aztecan ruler, seated on his majestic throne, greeted them as he would royalty. "O my beloved uncles. O merchants. You have suffered fatigue. Seat yourselves. Rest. The god Huitzilopochtli wished you to achieve your goals. Here I see you."

The merchants seated themselves. The nobles arranged themselves before their ruler according to their rank. In front sat the old men, with honored ones among them. Next sat the war chiefs. Then the seasoned warriors.

The merchants replied, "O our lord, may it be well with you. Behold the reward of the heads and breasts of thy beloved uncles, the merchants, who were captured in warlike places and killed. These goods we brought are the reward of their starvation, their fatigue. Accept these things in their names."

The ruler protested that the goods belonged to the merchants. But the merchants had their carriers open bundles, which held quetzal feathers made into headdresses, fans of feathers of rare birds, arm bands inlaid with precious stones, brace-

lets and rings, turquoise mosaic shields, gold but-
terfly-shaped nose plugs, lip plugs, and huge
golden earplugs that reached to the shoulder.
The eyes of the noblemen opened wide as each
valued article was held up for everyone to see.

Now the ruler ordered from his storehouse
gifts for the merchants. Soon slaves came in, under the direction of the noblemen in charge,
bringing mantles with flower designs; colored
breechcloths; bundles of capes, woven of strips of
rabbit fur, for winter wear; and also loads of corn
and beans and dried chili for the merchants to
take home. The goods the merchants brought
were placed in a storeroom. Eventually, as events
called for them, some would be distributed to
noblemen and warriors as gifts from the ruler for
their bravery and for service to the empire.

The noblemen left, and only the ruler and the
four supreme chiefs remained for a secret talk
with the merchants. Reading from a sheet of paper to refresh his memory, the spokesman for the
merchants began a report of the regions they
had visited, their populations, their wealth in in-
dividual products, and the size of their armies.

This was recorded for the ruler. When the Aztecan priests needed more captives for sacrifice, it might be well to attack one of these regions, to get captives and collect tribute.

There were long periods during the Aztecan Empire without war. Many merchants were on the roads, trading and spying. Until their return it was not wise to start a war. Yet captives were needed for sacrifices. Then the Aztec ruler announced a War of Flowers. The war chiefs of several cities were notified by special messengers. They agreed to select the best of their warriors for the battle, which was to take place on a set day. In one of these Wars of Flowers the very finest warriors of Tenochtitlán and their allies, men of Texcoco and Tlacopán, fought the warriors of Tlaxcala, an ancient Aztec enemy, and their allies, the men of Cholula and Huexotcingo. The warriors gladly accepted the challenge, because a captured warrior, whether Tlaxcalan, Cholulan, or Tlacopán, was glad to be sacrificed to the Sun God in order to live forever in the heavens in the company of the great. At the end of the contest those who were killed were quickly placed on the burning fires in the temple courtyard, for the Aztec usually burned the dead.

At one time a captive Tlaxcalan warrior named Tlahuicol was about to be sacrificed, when the Aztec Eagle and Tiger Warriors held a festival in honor of the sun. At the end of the festival these warriors enacted the daily battle between the Sun God and the God of Darkness. The captive Tlaxcalan was asked to fight the Aztec warriors before he was sacrificed. If he was victorious in this battle he would become their war chief—a very great honor.

According to custom, the Tlaxcalan was bound to the sacrificial altar in the temple courtyard—his arms left free for defense. Four warriors were selected to battle with him. These warriors had spears with sharp obsidian blades—as sharp as a steel knife. The captive was given only a blunt spear, covered with feathers, and a shield. But the brave Tlahuicol, using his spear as a foil, fended off the four warriors and tired them out. A fifth warrior then came to finish him, but Tlahuicol fought him off, too. Whereupon, the priest of the temple ruled that the brave captive would not be sacrificed, and he was set free.

The Aztecan war chiefs then asked Tlahuicol to lead an Aztec army in battle. This Tlahuicol did. He returned victorious with many captives, who would eventually be sacrificed, too. But in return for this service to the Aztec, he begged to be allowed to die on the sacrificial altar. Tlahuicol believed that the gods had wanted him to be captured in the first place, so he would be sacrificed. And he did not want to go against the wishes of the gods. After much pleading, the Aztecan priests complied with his request.

At the next ceremony to the Sun God, four priests held Tlahuicol's arms and legs and placed him on his back on the large stone altar. With a swift motion, a fifth priest, dressed in red, plunged his obsidian knife into Tlahuicol's strong body, tore out his heart, and held it up to the god Huitzilopochtli. Tlahuicol's crumpled body tumbled down the high temple steps. In the courtyard a fire had been lighted, and his remains were placed on the hot coals.

4

TO HONOR THE GODS

NUMEROUS ceremonies were carried out each
sacred year in the many temples of the Aztec. To
the Aztecans the year must have seemed like a
continuous pageant of preparations and sacrifices,
prayers, penance and pain, feasting, dancing, and
singing. All this was in honor of the various gods.
There were over a hundred such deities by now,
and the people spoke of each festival as a time to
pay a debt. But the people themselves never en-

Quetzalcoatl -- God of Wind

tered a temple. During a festival they gathered at the foot of the building, looked up, and watched the priests' activities.

In charge of all these events were three high priests. Two of them served the two highest gods —the War and Sun God, which we already know as Huitzilopochtli, and Tláloc, the Rain God. The third priest was in charge of all other religious activities within the Aztec Empire. Under

Huitzilopochtli

the third priest were two assistants, who supervised the instruction in the Aztecan schools and
kept an eye on the other temple priests. Each temple priest, in turn, had many assistants, including
students from the Cálmecac and young graduate
priests. It is said that there were 5000 assistants
during rituals at the Great Temple of Huitzilopochtli. All priests were called Tlamacazqui in
Nahuatl.

A priest's life was also filled with prayer, penance, and pain. The temples and the gods needed continuous attention. Incense had to be burned at specified hours, day and night. The temples had to be kept in order. They had to be in good repair both inside and outside. The gods, too, had to be painted and repainted.

Priests also served the people, as teachers of religion, as interpreters of the acts of the gods, and as directors at festivals. They saw to it that the religious rites were strictly observed. Since each priest represented the god he served, he wore clothes similar to those of his god. During rituals, a priest, dressed as a particular god, enacted for large audiences legendary episodes from the life of that god. These performances were often very dramatic, and they impressed vividly on the minds of the people details about their god's life, his deeds, his power, his greatness.

To honor Quetzalcoatl the creator, young actors played the roles of sick people. They limped up the temple steps or were carried there to be cured. Many added comedy to their complaints of ailments and made the audience laugh. Other priests portrayed animals. They climbed up trees and made funny faces at the crowd. Their stories, too, were often comical, to make people laugh.

Even though they attended many festivals and received continuous instruction, most Aztecs were quite vague as to the exact powers and functions of each of their gods. They, therefore, preferred to pray to their local village god, and begged him to protect them from all evil powers and to give them the things they needed—good crops, children, and health. Even in the cities, where people attended the temple rituals and did penance regularly, they were not always sure what was involved in each ceremony and left it entirely to the priests to guide them in exact observance.

According to the priests, the parents of the gods had four sons. Each son was given one of the four parts of the world to control. The fifth part of the world, the heavens above and the earth below, was left in the control of the parent gods. The father god ruled the heavens; the mother god ruled the earth. The earth was always in control of a female goddess, because it gave birth to crops, fruits, and trees.

Red Tezcatlipoca -- Xipe

Black Tezcatlipoca -- God of the Smoky Mirror

The first son, the red god Tezcatlipoca, controlled the East. In Aztecan writing, the color for the East was red. That is why Tezcatlipoca dressed in a red mantle. He was also called Xipe (Shee'-pay). The priests who impersonated Xipe wore the skin of a newly sacrificed person.

The next brother was the Black Tezcatlipoca, also known as the God of the Smoky Mirror. He controlled the North, and the North in Aztecan writing was always shown as black. So it was easy to recognize the Black Tezcatlipoca. He was painted with soot and with tiny metallic particles, which shone like a mirror. That was why he was also known as the God of the Smoky Mirror. Black Tezcatlipoca had lost his right foot, and instead of a sandal he had a round disc—another smoky mirror.

The third brother was the gentle god Quetzalcoatl, the God of Wind and the creator of mankind. He was also the God of Wisdom and Goodness and, as such, was worshiped by the Toltec and Mayan Indians. He had the beautiful blue-green feathers of the quetzal bird in his headdress and wore the mask of a serpent. Quetzalcoatl was originally the god of the Cholula Indians. At the city of Cholula a temple was built to him long before the Aztec came into power. The remains of this temple can be seen at Cholula today.

The fourth son of the parent gods was Huitzilopochtli, the God of War and the Sun God. He was the god of the South and was always shown in blue. The Aztec also referred to him as the Hummingbird Wizard. He led them to greatness and, therefore, remained their supreme god. Daily, accompanied by the serpents of fire, which were the sun's rays, Huitzilopochtli stepped into his glistening litter—which was Tonatiuh, the sun itself—and was carried across the sky by the spirits of warriors who had been sacrificed. At day's end the spirits of young mothers who had died in childbirth took the litter on their shoulders and carried it toward darkness. There Huitzilopochtli met with the gods of darkness and fought them, only to be defeated. Thus he was forced down to the worlds under the earth, to light them during the night. In the morning, however, the War God beat the gods of darkness and emerged again with the shining serpents, the shiny litter, and the spirits of warriors to carry him across the sky. These daily battles used up the god's energy. So the Aztecans had to keep sacrificing captives to feed him.

According to Aztecan beliefs, there were four ages of man. Each age died out when the sun died. At the end of the first age, as the sun died, there was a flood, and mankind turned into fish. At the end of the second age, mankind was swept off the earth by fire and turned into birds. At the end of the third age, the wind came and changed mankind into monkeys. The men of the fourth age were giants, and when the sun died they were consumed by jaguars.

As the fifth sun was born and mounted the sky, Quetzalcoatl, who loved mankind, went down into the worlds below and gathered the bones of the dead giants, which were badly mangled by the jaguars. But Quetzalcoatl pierced his own body and sprinkled his own blood over the bones he had gathered. They came to life and became the ancestors of the Aztec, as well as of all mankind. The Aztec were grateful that Quetzalcoatl had used his own blood to create them, and they tried to repay this debt with human sacrifice to feed him and the other gods. But the kind Quetzalcoatl evidently tired of wars and sacrifice, so he left Mexico.

To the farmers of Teotihuacán—a civilization that developed before the Aztec—the Rain God, Tláloc, was even more important than their creator Quetzalcoatl. The Aztec farmers remained grateful to Tláloc, and farmers everywhere prayed to him. He had the largest temple in

Tlaloc -- God of Rain

Tenochtitlán. The Aztec believed that in the mountains that surrounded them there were hidden caves, filled with water. Tláloc was in control of these caves, and little dwarfs lived in them. They gardened, just as the Aztec did, and kept the water for themselves. But after prayer and sacrifices to Tláloc—sometimes children were sacrificed when there were no captive warriors—the god ordered the dwarfs to carry rain to the Aztecan fields. The dwarfs, carrying small gourds filled with water, spread all over the sky and spilled the water over the land. When angered, Tláloc might send down hail and storms, or he might withhold all water and let the Aztecan fields dry up.

Tláloc always wore a headdress of white heron feathers. They were like the feathery cumulus clouds, which so often hover over the Valley of Mexico, promising rain. He was painted blue, like the sky and water.

His wife, Chalchihuitlicue, the Goddess of Green Skirts, ruled over the seas and lakes. The Aztec, since they were lake dwellers, prayed to her and honored her, too.

Some of the other gods were:

CINTEOTL and CHICOMECOATL, the god and goddess of corn

XILONEN, YOUNG CORN MOTHER, goddess of the young corn

XOCHIPILLI, the Prince of Flowers, the god in charge of dances, games, and love

METZTLI, the Moon God

MIXCOATL, Cloud Serpent, god of stars

ITZPAPALOTL, goddess of growing crops

TEPEYOLLOTI, Jaguar God, god of the mountains

YACATECUHTLI, the Lord Who Guides, god of the merchants

Everything that lives must die, so there were also a god and goddess of death, Mictlantecuhtli and his wife Mictlancihuatl. There was no mistaking the death god's appearance. His dress was covered with human bones. On his face was a skull. His black hair was covered with many eyes, so he could see in the dark underworlds where he lived. His necklace was made of human bones, and his earplug was a bone, too. His helpers were the bat, the spider, and the owl. If an Aztecan heard the call of an owl at night, it might bring death.

But death was not looked upon with fear. To the Aztec, it was the inevitable end that led to better worlds, provided, of course, a person died in the proper manner. There were thirteen heavens above and nine worlds underground. To the heavens went all brave warriors who died in battle. A special place was set aside for sacrificed enemy warriors. To heaven also went people who died of disease, by drowning, or when struck by lightning. All mothers who died in childbirth went to heaven because of their suffering on earth.

Life in the heavens was all songs and dancing. There was ample food and fruit. The seasoned warriors became the companions of the Sun God and helped him in his daily battles with the powers of darkness. But after four years some of these warriors returned to the earth as beautiful birds. There were always enough spirits in the heavens to enable the gods to create mankind again if it were ever destroyed.

But people who died in infancy or of old age had a hard time ahead of them in the nine worlds underground. An infant had not suffered enough on earth, and an old man must have had little sickness or suffering in order to reach old age. Their relatives buried them with many amulets and charms to see them through these difficult days. They flexed the knees of the body so it assumed a squatting position, and wrapped it tightly in a long piece of cotton. Paper was wrapped into the bundle, to make passage lighter and easier from one underworld to the next. The relatives burned the deceased's clothing, so the warmth from the fire would keep him warm while he was passing through some of the cold underworlds. They put a jade bead into the dead person's mouth, so that when the spirits underground tried to steal his heart, they would take the valuable bead instead. When it was believed that the deceased had gone through the tortures of all the nine underworlds and was starting upward toward the heavens, the relatives burned the body. The trip to the heavens took four years. Throughout this long period relatives made offerings to the gods to make the journey easier.

When a merchant died on a journey, presumably killed by an enemy, he, too, was destined to live among the warriors in heaven. His family made a paper image to resemble him and took it to their temple. They cried and prayed for a day. In the evening the paper image was burned. The merchant's spirit now soared safely heavenward.

A very special event, which ended with a sacrificial ceremony during the fifth month of the solar year—the month of Toxcatl in the spring—honored Black Tezcatlipoca, the God of the Smoky Mirror. A handsome young captive was selected by the priests to play the part of this god for an entire year. Such an honor was unsurpassed. The priests taught the captive youth about the god, as well as manners and behavior that befitted a divine being. They taught him Aztecan history. They taught him songs and how to play the flute.

The young god was dressed in the most beautiful breechcloths, mantles, and sandals. His jewelry was of gold and precious stones. He even smoked a gold pipe. His house of stone was decorated with gold and silver and precious stones, as befitted a god. Always, he carried flowers with him. Servants waited on him, played games with him, and carried him about in a shiny litter. When people saw him in the temple plaza they stopped in reverence. They gave the youth the same respect they showed before Tezcatlipoca's image at the temple.

After he had finished his preparations and schooling, the young man married four of the most beautiful maidens in Tenochtitlán. From his wives he received additional reverence. They prepared his food and accompanied him on his trips through the plaza and to the temple.

Then came spring and the month of Toxcatl. On the last day of the month the youth and his wives were taken in a royal canoe to a temple on the shore of the lake. They left him there with only a few attendants. Alone, the youth walked up the tall temple steps, where the priests were waiting for him. As he walked up, he broke, one after another, the clay pipes on which he had played during the year. When he reached the top, the priests stripped him of his rich mantle and breechcloth and laid him on the sacrificial stone. Four priests, dressed in black, held his arms and legs. A fifth priest, dressed in red, plunged his flint knife into the youth's body and tore out his heart. The priests carried the victim's head down the steps of the temple and placed it on a rack where the skulls of his predecessors were hung. The next day another captive youth was selected by the priests to be Tezcatlipoca for the following year.

While the Sun God lived forever, the Aztec believed that the sun itself, called Tonatiuh, died every 52 years. To keep track of the years, they adopted two calendars. One was their sacred calendar, which was made up of 20 months of 13 days each. The other, which was devised by the learned Aztecan astronomers after years of studying the heavens and the movements of the stars and planets, was made up of 20 months of 18 days each, or 360 days. Another 5 days were added at the year's end to make up 365 days. Each month a different god was honored with a festival.

The last five days at the end of a fifty-two-year cycle might bring disaster. During these five days the Aztec fasted, prayed, and did penance. They waited for a catastrophe. Pregnant mothers were shut up in storerooms, so they would not be changed into wild animals. Children were not allowed to go to sleep. Were a child to fall asleep, it would never awaken, so they were kept awake with the help of all sorts of noisemakers.

When the sun set on the fatal 365th day, the priests of Tenochtitlán, dressed in the costumes of the gods, climbed the Hill of the Star, which was an extinct crater. There they kept vigil during the night. In the meantime, householders had let their fires go out. They broke their used pots and threw out their old mats and clothing. Everyone waited in deep darkness. As the night passed and people remained alive and were not devoured by monsters, they began to hope that all would be well and that a new sun would be born and begin a new fifty-two-year cycle.

The priests began to work their fire drill over prepared wood shavings, which had been stuffed into the body of a newly sacrificed person. Runners were ready to light their torches and start new fires at the temples. From these, people lit their torches and carried them home to light the kitchen fires. Happiness overwhelmed the land.

The Aztec now considered themselves safe from a major calamity for the next fifty-two years. People rushed about getting dressed in their best clothes. Homes were redecorated, and new pots and mats were brought out for the new year. People feasted. They punctured their ear lobes and tongues and smeared their blood on the altars of the gods in thanksgiving for having been saved. Girls and women rushed out into the fields to pick flowers with which to fill their homes for the festivities. Relatives visited one another, bringing gifts and carrying away gifts in return. The Sun God once again rode in his shiny litter across the sky.

Each temple ceremony had games and dances. The ball game the Aztec played was the same as that played by the Mayan Indians. The Aztec game also had a sacred meaning, because it was played in a temple court for the enjoyment of the gods as well as of the people. The players were usually of the nobility.

The ball court consisted of three fields laid out in a peculiar H shape. The center field of the H was longer than the side fields. A ball player had to be an expert to survive, for the ball was of hard, solid rubber, and when it hit a player accidentally it left a deep bruise. That is why each player wore a wide belt, a heavy leather apron, and also pads on the arms, thighs, and knees. The ball was never touched with the hands. A player tossed it with his elbows, knees, and hips, and aimed to knock it from one field to another. There were two baskets overhead, one on each side of the center bar. It was considered a feat to get the ball through one of the baskets. When a player succeeded in doing this, the game ended, and he was the victor.

The dances at a temple must have been colorful and gay at all times, in view of the multicolored, embroidered mantles and the headdresses of the public. The music was produced by drums, noisemakers, flutes, and conch-shell trumpets. When a very big crowd had gathered, the older noblemen, as well as the most important people, formed a close circle around the altar in the temple court- yard. As the music played, they moved slowly and with great dignity around and around the altar. A second and much larger circle was then formed of people who were mature but who had more energy than the oldsters in the first circle. This second circle moved faster in time to the music. A third circle was made up of very young dancers, who pranced about gaily with speed and rhythm and laughter.

The dance of the Four Earthquakes was cele- brated to honor the sun, Tonatiuh. The Aztec be- lieved that the present sun would be destroyed by earthquakes. A captive, dressed like the sun, climbed a platform on which a huge stone bearing the face of the sun was set. There he was sacrificed to Tonatiuh. This stone, which can be seen today at the Museum of Anthropology and History in Mexico City, weighs over twenty tons and is over twelve feet in diameter. It is called the Calen- dar Stone. Various calculations indicate that the carving of the stone began in 1479 under the

Aztecan ruler, Axayacatl. The stone was quarried far inland and pulled on stone rollers over miles and miles of trails to its destination in Tenochtitlán. Skilled stoneworkers and sculptors worked with small stone mallets, obsidian, and bone chisels to engrave this giant stone in honor of the sun.

In its center is the face of Tonatiuh. His hands, which are eagle claws, are on the same level as his face, and in each hand he clutches a human heart. Four squares surround Tonatiuh's face. These are four calendar dates of four other suns, which died at the end of each previous fifty-two-year cycle. A band surrounds Tonatiuh's face and hands. On it are engraved the signs of the days. Two other bands are the two fire serpents, which are the sun's rays.

The colorful dance of the Eagle and Tiger Warriors followed the Four Earthquakes ceremony. At the end of this dance, the Eagle and Tiger Warriors fought the captive who was to be sacrificed to Tonatiuh.

There was also a dance to honor the Fire God. The Fire God priests were the dancers. They placed bound captives on their backs and carried them around and around the blazing fires in the temple courtyard. The captives' hearts were first taken out and offered to the god before their bodies were thrown into the flames.

To all these ceremonies, the audiences also added their small share of pain and sacrifice. Each person pricked his skin and offered drops of blood to the gods. This, they believed, was what the gods demanded in order that the Aztec might continue their success in war, as befitted a chosen people.

5

SUCCESS

By 1503, when Montezuma ascended the Aztec throne, Tenochtitlán and Tlaltelolco were indeed impressive towns. The population of Tenochtitlán has been estimated as low as 60,000 and as high as 300,000, with thousands of homes, many magnificent temples, and the palaces of the ruler. All of the finest workmanship in the Aztec Empire flowed into Tenochtitlán by loaded canoes and by human carriers over the busy causeways. The city was crowded, since there was no ready room for expansion. But the Aztec and their slaves con-

tinued enlarging the shores and adding more
ground by means of the old chinampas, or floating gardens.

The plazas of Tenochtitlán and Tlaltelolco remained the main parts of the towns. In the evening people went up on the flat roof tops, as many
do today in crowded cities, to enjoy the cool evening air and to watch the goings on in the busy
thoroughfares, in the canals, and on the causeways. The smooth white houses nestled among the
trees; the colorful patios in the midst of each
group of buildings were filled with flowers, birds,
and playing children. Their temples loomed high
above the trees, for temples of unconquerable gods
should meet the sky.

To the noblemen, this, their precious city,
added to their pride, like a valued piece of jadeite
or a bundle of quetzal feathers. It was a great
achievement in engineering and architecture and
was entirely theirs. The Aztec looked about and
saw the blue waters that enclosed their green island, and felt safe. For a warlike people to feel
safe is important. No enemy from the mainland
could get near them without being seen immedi-

ately. There were no land routes to Tenochtitlán except the causeways, which could be closed by raising drawbridges.

At all hours, day and night, silent canoes glided over the lake, bringing food and raw materials to the town. Each group of buildings had its own wharf, where the canoes tied up and were unloaded by waiting slaves. The men and women in the canoes, even though tired from their long paddling, were anxious to take a look at the life of the big town. They watched the people on their roofs, dressed in their rich mantles and feathered headdresses. Their eyes then turned to the temples where the gods dwelt. They believed their gods must be rich to live in such magnificent places, and this made them feel less humble, even though they were only dressed in simple whitecotton breechcloths and huipils.

A procession of priests was on the way to the temple. They wore bright mantles, designed to match the dress of their gods. The men and women in the canoes watched them mount the steps of the temple. No one except the priesthood ever got beyond the bottom steps. No one else entered a temple and faced his god at eye level. Always, the gods soared high above.

Visitors to Tenochtitlán from another city were coming over a causeway. A merchant was returning, still dressed in the plain maguey mantle he had worn while on the road. A nobleman in a litter, carried by four slaves, was returning from far away. Behind him were many carriers, bent under their heavy loads. As they passed a farmer and his wife, sitting in a canoe, began to count the carriers in twenties as they were taught. They repeated the count five times—five times twenty, or a hundred carriers.

The list of tributes brought in was carefully recorded in the palace book. One such list shown on the books read:

20 gourd dishes of gold dust
a royal headdress
800 bunches of feathers
40 bags of cochineal dye
warriors' costumes
16,006 blankets, each in a different pattern

But the empty canoes had to leave the dock.

Other canoes were coming in, getting ready to unload. For a moment the canoemen envied the carriers, who worked harder, but who could drop their burdens and remain in the city for a while. In the shade of a tree they were able to watch important people and priests at close range. But the canoemen had more work to do. The next day they might stay over at the market place in Tlaltelolco, where they would talk, feast, drink pulque, and really mix and mingle with the people.

Since the palace of Montezuma received a thorough inspection from the Spanish conquerors, we have eyewitness descriptions of its contents. The palace consisted of many rooms and, like the temples, was built on several levels. The ground floor had chambers for the war council and the justices. The second story, above it, was narrower, allowing room for a terrace on three sides. Here were rooms reserved for visiting allied chiefs. To impress the visitors, these rooms were decorated with rich hangings, pottery, vases, masks and shields, inlaid with turquoise and shell, and sculpture from different parts of the Aztecan domain. A tall stairway led to a third, still narrower story. Here were Montezuma's chambers and the large sumptuous throne room where he received visitors.

The living quarters of the palace spread to other buildings. There were separate dwellings for Montezuma's many wives and children. The buildings faced lovely patios and gardens, filled with flowers and herbs. The rooms were large and richly decorated. Montezuma had a special area built for his zoo, where animals from all over America were fed and housed. There was a special aviary with large cages. The colorful birds of Central and South America were housed here. Among them were the rare quetzal birds, which grow only two long and slender green-blue feathers in their tails. These, the caretakers plucked from time to time, and the birds, well cared for, grew more feathers.

There were also humbler buildings housing the servants, the court craftsmen and their families, and the jesters, acrobats, and dwarfs, who entertained the ruler, his circle of noblemen, and honored guests. The wealth of the Aztecan rulers filled many storerooms, which were well guarded.

Careful lists of their bulging contents were kept by special men.

It is said that meals prepared daily at the palace served several hundred people. While the food of the average farming family was plain and simply cooked, there were some 2000 different dishes prepared daily in Montezuma's banquet hall. Even here the mainstay of a meal was the large tortilla. Since only plates were used—no spoons or knives—the tortilla served as a scoop for food that could not be picked up with the fingers. Tortillas were served hot off the griddles, and there were several kinds. Some were thin and fine; others, thick; some were folded; some were rolled.

There were corncakes, or steamed tamales, made of crushed corn, mixed with beans and peppers. The Nahuatl word for this dish is *tamalli*, and it is now known as tamale in Mexico and wherever there is Mexican cooking. The tamales were stuffed with meat or chopped turkey or quail.

Chili is another Nahuatl word. Chili peppers were grown in a variety of shades, from bright green, red, or yellow, to very dark colors. Most dishes were flavored with chili, and all sauces had one or several kinds in them.

Tomatoes—*tomatl* in Nahuatl—were native to Central America in red and yellow varieties. As we do today, the Aztec crushed them into sauces, sliced them, and ate them raw, baked, or roasted.

Of meats there were fowl, birds of all kinds and sizes, venison, rabbit, gopher, and dog meat. The Aztec liked their turkey sliced and dipped in a special chili sauce, made with tomatoes and crushed squash seeds. They also roasted their turkeys and other meat or stewed them with peppers. Ducks and geese were roasted and dried. Dried duck, dipped in a pepper sauce, was a favorite dish.

Avocadoes—*ahuacatl*, another Nahuatl word—were also crushed with peppers and seeds to make a rich, tasty, nourishing dish called *guacamolé*. *Molé* itself is made with crushed red peppers.

Sea foods—fish, lobster, shrimp, and other shellfish—were eaten too. The Aztec also ate frogs' legs, tadpoles, and varieties of ants, locusts, and maguey grubs. Women gathered water greens of all kinds and crushed and boiled them as vegetables or made soups from them. They prepared squash blossoms, water cress, and scraped thistle fruit and used wild onions and garlic for flavoring. At every meal there were a few plates of ground beans, called frijoles (free-ho'-lays) in Spanish. The farmers grew several kinds of beans, which made a good substitute for meat. There were also sweet dishes, such as boiled or baked sweet potatoes, brown, juicy sweet sapotes, cactus fruits, wild cherries, plums, honey, and sugar cane. Children liked sweets and were happy to eat their tortillas dipped in honey.

Obviously Montezuma could not eat or even sample all of these dishes at any one time. He was of medium build and slender, and probably a moderate eater. But the warriors and his retinue of noblemen ate heartily. Leftovers were taken to the houses of the wives and the servants. Some of the food got cold and probably even spoiled by the time it reached the last consumer. The humblest servants probably preferred the hot tortillas their wives readied for their meal, and scooped up with them enough of the leftover sauces and frijoles to satisfy their hunger.

The food and produce came to the palace by canoe and by carriers over the causeways from the mainland. Some of it came from the farms and fields that belonged to the royal family. The nobility, too, had fields of their own and stored the harvest in their own storehouses.

Additional foods and other household needs were purchased in the markets. The large plaza of Tlaltelolco was reserved for a market place. The bustle of activity began with the dawn. Some people had walked for days, carrying their trade goods to Tlaltelolco's famous market. Each person went first to that part of the market place where his particular produce or wares were on display. This was important, because each was anxious to get a good spot for himself, spread his mats, and arrange his goods in an attractive display. If the spot would be sunny later in the day, he tied a piece of cloth on four posts, so he could sit in the shade and trade in comfort.

The Tlaltelolco market, like the large market places in Mexico today, was divided into sections according to the type of goods displayed. There were special sections for pottery, for example.

Potters from all over the Aztec Empire brought their best wares to sell. Pots, bowls, plates, and griddles were of many colors, glazes, shapes, and types of artistry. Most were hand-painted, since even the humblest pot seemed pleasanter to handle if it was well made. There were special sections for baskets and mats, for rope and burden straps, or tumplines. Here, too, the variety was staggering, and there was much craftsmanship to admire. That is why so many people came to the market just to look at the wares. Even the simple maguey tumplines, which the carriers used to steady their burdens, were filled with color and design.

The food section was divided into areas where different varieties of corn, beans, peanuts, and other items were displayed. Measures were standardized, and the price for each measure was set. There were heaps of fresh greens and vegetables and peppers, arranged in little handfuls for a housewife to purchase. There were fruits, nuts, and sweets. Montezuma's cooks could select here all they needed for the daily meals at his table.

Butchered meat was on sale in special places.

In others, the housewife could buy live turkeys, ducks, or birds and slaughter them herself when she got home, so the meat would be fresh. Fishermen from the lakes displayed their morning catch in the section assigned to sea food. They placed the fish on large green banana leaves to make it more attractive to the housewife. There were dried fish as well as fresh fish, shellfish, and shrimp. There were turtle eggs, duck eggs, and birds' eggs.

Beautiful cotton cloth was for sale, along with finished mantles, breechcloths, and leather sandals, fit for the finest noblemen. There were simple breechcloths and mantles of cotton and maguey and huipils for women.

In other sections craftsmen had their wares on display—carved and lacquered wooden bowls and trays, stone carvings, metates and manos (hand stones) for grinding corn at home. Even the simple flat-bottomed canoes used by the farmers and fishermen were on display. In a nearby section silversmiths displayed their wares, which only the nobility could afford to buy. The Aztec valued silver more than gold, because silver was harder to obtain and harder to shape than gold.

There was also a place for selling all kinds of flowers, some cultivated, some wild. And in all the sections, women set up their hot griddles on a few stones and kept small fires under them. They offered freshly fried fish and sauces to be rolled in hot tortillas, which they patted into shape for a waiting customer. There were also many places where men could purchase pulque.

From early morning on, customers of all classes filled the market place. They wandered from section to section, looking, admiring, trading, and buying. Farmers and farm women, their babies tied over their shoulders in wide cotton shawls with little bundles of food and cacao beans knotted in front, pointed out the sights to their children, explaining and educating them in the marvels of the big city. Noblewomen, followed by slaves carrying baskets, looked at everything, too, pricing the items they wished for their households.

Trading in the early days was an exchange of goods. For a gourdful of corn a woman exchanged a pot she had made, or she might buy a few pieces of fruit or sugar cane for her children. For small items the cacao bean, which was used by all, became a unit of exchange. For very large purchases thin copper knives, shaped like a crescent moon, and even gold dust were used.

At day's end the people began to fold and put away their goods. Some loaded canoes. Others carried the unsold goods to warehouses in the city. The craftsmen, with the help of their wives and children, carried the unsold articles home. No one was disappointed at not having sold enough, because there would be many more market days and the people were glad to have things to sell.

6

CONQUEST

MONTEZUMA, the last ruler of the Aztec Empire, was a seasoned soldier, war chief, and conqueror. He ruled during the most turbulent times of the empire. Uprisings flared up among the Texcoco and among the Tlaxcala in the southeast, and Montezuma had to fight them. But neither he nor his predecessors ever succeeded in subduing the Tlaxcalans entirely, as they had the Zapotecans of Oaxaca. Nor did they conquer the Tarascan Indians of Michoacán. Even though he needed manpower for further wars, Montezuma continued mass sacrifices, because, above all, he was a religious man who believed in the power of the gods and his debt to them. Although he was still young, he may also have believed that the time was coming—as predicted by the court magicians—for his reign to end.

When Montezuma learned that a boat with strange men had landed on the Gulf coast, he sent five scouts to investigate. To avoid the suspicion that they were scouts for Montezuma, the men brought with them mantles of varied design—the sun design, the design of a blue serpent, a mask design, and a smoky-mirror design. The scouts planned to say that they were merchants, who had come to trade.

The scouts boarded the Spanish ship, marveling at its size and construction. Never had they seen a boat so huge, nor one holding so many people and horses, which the Aztecans called deer in Nahuatl. As they boarded the ship, they kissed the prow, convinced that a canoe of this size was certainly made by the gods and that the figurehead on the prow was a carved image of Quetzalcoatl.

The Spaniards accepted the mantles. They dug into their possessions and came up with a few handfuls of glass beads—cheap green-and-yellow necklaces. They told the merchants that they had not come to stay but were returning to Castile, their native land.

The messengers left the ship in their canoes and hastily walked overland day and night to reach Tenochtitlán with the good tidings that the gods were not coming to Mexico to stay. They said to Montezuma, "We went to see our lords, the gods, in the midst of the ocean. All thy mantles we gave them. Behold, they gave us these noble goods. They said, 'If in truth you are from Mexico, this you shall give the ruler Montezuma. Then he will know us.' "

Montezuma begged the messengers to keep their information secret, so the people would not be frightened.

The palace craftsmen, who had never seen glass before, studied the necklaces with deep interest. The glass resembled in texture the smoky obsidian that they used in making knives and spear points, but the necklaces were much clearer.

It must be a new kind of valuable turquoise the gods had created. Montezuma, therefore, ordered the gifts stored away for safekeeping for the gods.

Another year went by. At Montezuma's orders, the coast was well watched. When the Spanish ships returned in 1519, with Hernan Cortes in one of them, Montezuma was immediately notified. Again he sent a few of his noblemen to find out the gods' intentions. This time he sent the gods rich gifts. Among them were two complete costumes for Quetzalcoatl, one for the god Tezcatlipoca, and another for Tláloc, the Rain God. The Aztecan noblemen thought Cortes was the god Quetzalcoatl. They found out too late that the Spanish government had sent him to conquer Mexico.

The noblemen dressed Cortes in one of Quetzalcoatl's costumes and laid out the other costumes for him to see. They dressed him in a rich mantle, decorated with a wide border of shiny feathers. On his face, they put Quetzalcoatl's serpent mask, which was inlaid with turquoise. They placed a tall headdress of quetzal feathers on Cortes' head, and on his neck a choker of precious jade beads surrounding a large golden disc. They showed him how to balance on his left arm the shield, inlaid with bands of gold and quetzal feathers, with a polished obsidian mirror in its center. In his right hand, the noblemen placed a spear with a very fine, long obsidian point. They took off Cortes' shoes and substituted a pair of rare and valuable obsidian sandals.

When they had finished dressing him and laying out the treasure, a nobleman spokesman said to Cortes, as Montezuma had instructed him, "Behold what thy servant Montezuma has sent thee. Montezuma prays to thee, knowing that thou hast suffered and art weary of travel."

Marina, Cortes' Indian interpreter, stood beside him watching the ceremony. She explained the meaning of each part of the costume to Cortes and informed him that he had been accepted by the Aztec as the god Quetzalcoatl.

Marina, known to history as La Malinche, knew the religion of the Aztec. Her father had been a powerful chief. When he died, her mother remarried and bore a son. In order that the son might inherit her first husband's lands, the mother claimed her daughter was dead. Secretly, she gave Marina to a merchant and asked him to take her far away. The merchant sold Marina as a slave, and she was given to Cortes when he was welcomed by the Indians of the island of Ulua on the Gulf.

The young woman was intelligent and knew Nahuatl well. She quickly learned to speak Spanish and became Cortes' interpreter and later his Indian wife. As a wife, her loyalty belonged to her husband's people. She probably felt no remorse at betraying the Indian people to the strangers from across the ocean.

After Cortes ascertained that these were all the gifts the messengers brought, he ordered the noblemen seized and had chains clamped on their necks and ankles. He next ordered one of the large lombard cannons to be discharged. To the Aztec, this was a clap of thunder from the Rain God, which proved he was happy with the gifts.

Later the Spanish removed the chains and gave the Aztecans food. They suggested that the Aztec stay overnight aboard ship. Tomorrow the Spanish warriors would have a contest with the warriors of Montezuma. They had heard that the Aztecans were very brave. The noblemen begged to be allowed to go home, since Montezuma had not instructed them to enter into a contest with the gods. Cortes released them the following morning. The messengers scurried to their canoes and paddled away as fast as they could.

Again, after several days of walking, the noblemen reached the palace and gave Montezuma a detailed description of all that had happened to them, including the thunder they had heard from the gods, the strange food they had eaten, and the strong iron armor and weapons possessed by the Spaniards. They further reported that all had very white faces. Some of the gods' assistants had yellow hair; others had dark, curly hair. Their beards were as thick as their hair. They also had strange lean dogs with yellow eyes and fierce voices. These dogs seemed hungry. Mexican dogs were very different. They were all fat, since they were raised for meat, and they did not bark.

Montezuma immediately ordered two captives to be sacrificed in honor of the new gods. He called a council of his soothsayers and priests to get their advice on how to proceed with the strange gods. It was decided to carry food to them and thus court their favor. The cooks at the palace set about preparing their most attractive dishes. They loaded carriers with tortillas, meats, turkeys, ducks, eggs, honey, sweet potatoes, and peppers, as well as plums, guavas, and cactus fruits. The court magicians and priests accompanied these gifts.

Montezuma's spokesmen presented these foods to Cortes. The Spanish quickly turned away from the dishes, because the tortillas, the sauces, the fish, and the meat were sprinkled with the blood of the sacrificed captives. However, they ate the fruit.

In the meantime, unobserved, the magicians tried some of the magic they had found effective on their own people, but it did not work on the Spaniards. After they returned, the court magicians sadly reported to Montezuma, "We cannot fight these gods. We are as nothing against them."

News had already leaked out among the people. They said that an Indian woman was leading the gods to Mexico. Men, women, and children hid in their homes, wept, and cried out in despair, "What will happen to our sons and daughters?"

In the meantime, the Spaniards had landed and began their advance inland. They clashed with the Otomi Indians and almost wiped them out. The Tlaxcalans put up some resistance but also found the Spaniards too strong and their cannons too powerful. They surrendered and agreed to lead the Spaniards to Tenochtitlán against their old enemies, the Aztec. The journey to Mexico took three days. En route, the Spaniards entered Cholula, where Quetzalcoatl's first temple stood. The Spaniards ordered everyone to gather peacefully in the temple courtyard. The Cholulans obeyed and left their weapons behind. The Spaniards thereupon surrounded the courtyard and killed all the Cholulans and looted the temple and the deserted homes. They kept the gold and silver ornaments, but destroyed and burned everything else that held no value to them —leather artwork and featherwork, statues, ornaments, and pottery.

The Spaniards were now within sight of
Tenochtitlán. Again, Montezuma sent messengers with more rich gifts of golden streamers,
quetzal feathers, and necklaces. The small group
of Spaniards, with Cortes and Marina in the lead,
rode quickly over one of the causeways to meet
Montezuma. The causeways and waterways were
emptied of people. Tenochtitlán was like a city
of the dead. Watching the approaching armies
from inside their homes, the people cried, "Now
we shall die. We shall perish."

Montezuma awaited them in the plaza of
Tenochtitlán, which was then known as Xocolo
and is today called the Zócalo. He was surrounded by his nobles, princes, and chiefs.
Women from the palace had gathered flowers for
the occasion. They made the long-stemmed sunflowers, the white and yellow magnolias, and the
sweet-smelling cacao blossoms into garlands to
decorate the gods.

Montezuma was dressed in his finest feather
mantle and jewels. His tall headdress of some
400 shiny green quetzal feathers caught the rays
of the sun. The headdress made him a full head

taller than Cortes. Although he actually was a slender, olive-skinned man of average height, with a thin, tiny beard, he looked majestic and very impressive to Cortes.

Cortes dismounted and spoke in his strange tongue, which Marina interpreted into Nahuatl. "Are you Montezuma?"

If Montezuma had not believed all that the legends predicted, he would never have greeted Hernan Cortes as he did. Cortes had only 400 men, and Montezuma had no fear of his Tlaxcalan allies. He would surely have fought them had he doubted that Cortes was any other but the great god, Quetzalcoatl, returned to Mexico.

Montezuma's eloquent greeting was almost a prayer. He said to Cortes, "O our lord, thou hast suffered fatigue; thou hast spent thyself. Thou hast arrived on earth. Thou hast come to thy noble city of Mexico. Thou hast come to occupy thy noble mat and seat, which for a little time I have guarded and watched for thee. Thy governors of the past have gone. Gone are the rulers Itzcoatl, Montezuma the Elder, Axayacatl, Tizoc, Ahuitzotl.

"O that one of them might be a witness to marvel that to me now hath befallen what I see, who am the only descendant of our lords. This is not a dream. I am not starting from my sleep. I have gazed into the unknown whence thou hast come—the place of mystery. The rulers of old said that thou wouldst come to thy mat and seat. Now it is fulfilled. Arrive now in thy land. Rest, lord. Visit thy palace."

Cortes replied, and Montezuma listened as
Marina interpreted, "May Montezuma quiet his
heart and not be frightened. We love him much.
Now our hearts are satisfied, because we have
wanted to see him and look upon his face. And
now we have seen him and have come to his home
in Mexico. At leisure he may hear our words." As
Cortes spoke, he took Montezuma by the hand.
No one living was of equal rank to hold Montezuma's hand. But Cortes was a god.

Spanish horsemen dismounted and came over
for a closer look at the Aztecan king, as he and
Cortes began to walk toward the palace. Cortes
next slapped Montezuma on the back as a gesture
of Spanish friendship and again took his hand.
Little did Montezuma suspect that henceforth,
until he died in 1520, he would no longer know
freedom.

Montezuma had feared this meeting, since all
Aztecans feared their gods. They never knew
whether the gods would bring good or evil. From
Quetzalcoatl one might expect only good, even
though, as prophesied, he would take the Aztecan Empire away from Montezuma.

The looting of homes and temples began immediately. The Spanish soldiers tore the gold hangings, the gold ornaments, and the gold trimmings from the walls of the palace rooms and stuffed them into their pockets and saddlebags. They threw away and trampled underfoot everything else that had no gold or silver in it. They made a huge bonfire in the Zócalo and tossed Aztecan treasures into it. They set fire to the looted homes, but these, surrounded by water, did not burn readily.

Watching the looting, killing, and burning, and the frenzy of the Spaniards, the Aztec now knew that these were not gods but evil men. The Eagle and Tiger Warriors began in secret to organize the men in the towns and villages to fight this new enemy.

At Veracruz two Spaniards, who were caught looting, were slain by an Aztecan chief, governor of a neighboring province. Upon Cortes' cry for justice, Montezuma had the chief, his son, and fifteen warriors brought to the palace. But Cortes did not even listen to the Aztecans' just complaints, as he had promised Montezuma he would. Instead he immediately ordered them burned on a pyre in the center of the Zócalo, as a lesson to other rebels. This, of course, did not stop the Aztec.

Cortes was a resourceful enemy. He wished to destroy this great civilization, but he underestimated the spirit and courage of the Aztecans. Therefore, he had to act fast, because the Tlaltelolco market now stood silent and empty. The farmers brought no produce, and his men could not eat the gold they looted. Cortes' threats to Montezuma were of no avail. He could not get the imprisoned ruler to order his people to feed the conquerors. The Spaniards faced starvation as well as destruction.

Bernal Diaz del Castillo, a twenty-seven-year-old soldier who fought with Cortes, wrote some fifty-seven years later about the conquest of Mexico and gave an eyewitness account of those turbulent days. Bernal Diaz wrote that never in all his campaigns had he seen such furious, fearless fighting. The cannons and muskets held no fear for the Aztecan warriors. As soon as a charge mowed down thirty or forty of them, another tight group of forty or fifty took their place. Time and again the Aztecans feigned retreat. When the Spaniards went after them, the warriors about-faced and attacked them. They fought night and day, shouting and whistling, giving the Spaniards no rest. They shouted that they would leave no Spaniard or Tlaxcalan alive. All would be sacrificed to the gods who watched over the Aztec.

Cortes' captains now threatened to revolt if he did not leave Mexico. Cortes then ordered Montezuma to speak to his people and to tell them to stop fighting, so the Spaniards could leave his country in peace. But Montezuma, according to Bernal Diaz, only replied, "I do not want to hear or see Cortes or Marina and listen to more promises and lies. My people have already chosen another lord and will not let you out alive." This lord was Cuauhtémoc (Kwo-tay'-mok), a war chief and a nephew of Montezuma. He was a fearless man, who hoped to continue the resistance and defeat the Spaniards.

Finally Cortes forced Montezuma to appear before his people. The fighting ceased when the warriors beheld their former ruler. A spokesman shouted to him, "O Lord, our great Lord, how greatly we are afflicted by our misfortune and that of your sons and relatives. We have already raised one of your kinsmen to be our lord. The fighting must go on till none of the enemy is left."

A fresh shower of arrows, spears, and stones followed. The defenseless Montezuma was hit by three stones. One struck him on the head, another on the arm, and a third on the leg. He refused to let the Spanish attend his wounds and died that day. Bernal Diaz recorded that even the Spanish soldiers wept on learning of Montezuma's death, the loss of a just and brave man.

Cortes then left Tenochtitlán for six months, and he put his lieutenant and companion-at-arms, Pedro de Alvarado, in charge. The time arrived for the important festival honoring the god of war Huitzilopochtli. The noblemen asked Alvarado's permission to celebrate this ceremony in the temple, which the Spaniards occupied. Alvarado granted permission. But when the people and nobility gathered in the Zócalo in front of the temple, Alvarado gave the signal to shoot at the crowd. Seeing the attack, men and women tried to escape, but the Spanish soldiers speared them.

The Aztec kept on fighting. The farmer warriors around Tenochtitlán manned canoes and surrounded the city. The Spanish tried to sneak out of the city at night, but the Aztec watched them. They cut the bridges on the causeways, so the soldiers and their Indian allies toppled into the canals. The Spanish, who were weighted with bags of loot, sank to the bottom. It is estimated that some 300 Spanish were thus killed and about 4000 of their Indian allies.

But the Aztecans did not pursue the fleeing enemy and destroy them completely, because that was not their way of waging war. Instead, they let the remnants of the Spanish army escape, and tried to save the valuable loot they had dropped.

The Spaniards made their way toward the lands of the Tlaxcalans, their allies. On the way, they were attacked by the Texcocans. The Texcocans, however, were no match for the Spanish cavalry. The Spanish horsemen charged and trampled the Texcocan war chiefs to death, and the Indians fled from the field of battle.

After rest and recovery, Cortes first concentrated on subduing the eastern part of Mexico. He again gathered thousands of Indian allies. He had boat parts constructed and ordered the Indians to carry them overland into the canals of Tenochtitlán and put them together there. Thus surrounded, the city had its food supply cut off. But under the leadership of the courageous Cuauhtémoc, the Aztecans did not give in. Each night canoemen sallied forth and destroyed the bridges over the causeways. The Spanish kept repairing the bridges and moving troops. Cortes next ordered his men to wreck the houses of Tenochtitlán and to dump the rubble into the canals, giving the Spanish more room to move.

For a time, however, it looked as though the Aztec would hold out, because they were promised help from their enemies, the Xochimilca. This Xochimilcan offer had aroused the Aztec's last hopes. Cuauhtémoc rushed valuable gifts of mantles, precious ornaments, and cacao beans to the Xochimilcan chiefs. But the Xochimilca proved traitors. They filtered into Tenochtitlán at night and captured Aztecan women and children to carry off as slaves. The Aztecans had to fight them off, as well as the Spanish.

By now they were too exhausted by war and lack of food to resist the ever-pressing Spaniards. Cuauhtémoc surrendered, on the promise that his life would be spared. But Cortes, as might be expected, took Cuauhtémoc with him after the Aztecans were defeated. Once out of the city, he hanged him.

The Spaniards then set about to rebuild the ruins of Tenochtitlán, which was now called Mexico City. The temple of Tláloc in the Zócalo was demolished. On its foundation a cathedral, which still stands today, arose. The stones from the other temples, from the palaces and noblemen's homes were used in building houses for the conquerors. Any leftover materials were dumped into the canals as fill. The skilled Aztec stonemasons were now working under the whip of Spanish overseers. They liked the new steel and iron tools, the chisels, saws, and hammers, and began to turn out excellent durable work, which can still be seen today, more than four centuries later.

The lands of Mexico were divided among the Spanish conquerors. Indians who were not killed or imprisoned for rebelling became slaves of the Spanish. They worked the large plantations, or haciendas, for their Spanish masters. They were recruited into mines. They tended the ever-growing herds of cattle, sheep, goats, hogs, and horses, which the Spanish brought to Mexico. Long stretches of cornfields, once so carefully irrigated and cultivated, gave way to wheat fields, because the Spanish were used to wheat bread. Wheat could also be shipped to Europe as a cash crop. Other cornfields were turned into pastures for the cattle.

It is reported that $200,000 in smelted gold brick alone was shipped by Cortes to the Spanish king. He also shipped Aztecan art to Spain, including a large sun made entirely of gold, a moon made of silver, and all sorts of weapons and rich mantles. The cotton armor the Aztecan soldiers used found such favor that soon the Spanish soldiers were wearing it, too.

Montezuma's carefully made headdress of quetzal feathers eventually found its way to Vienna, Austria, as a gift to a friend from the court of Spain. But a copy of it is now on display in the Museum of Anthropology and History in Mexico City. Even this copy is a distinguished work of art.

In 1520 the great European artist and painter, Albrecht Dürer, saw some of the Aztecan treasures in Spain and exclaimed, "I have never seen in all my days what so rejoiced my heart as these things. Amazing artistic objects—subtle ingenuity of men in distant lands."

7

THE AZTEC TODAY

THROUGH a series of uprisings, caused by poverty and by the oppression of the Spanish landlords, the people of Mexico finally overthrew the foreign yoke. It took over four hundred years to achieve this. The country was torn and bled through revolutions and civil war. Finally Mexico emerged as a nation. The majority of its people were still poor, but they were filled with hope for the future. The Aztec and other Indian groups survived. In Mexico today they are over ten million strong. In the villages of Mexico the Aztecans have retained their Nahuatl language, and many still speak it as their only language. They are farmers, herdsmen, traders, weavers, and craftsmen.

Since Mexico is our close neighbor, anyone from the United States of the North is welcome to visit the United States of Mexico—or simply Mexico, as we call that country—and see it for himself. People from all over the world visit Mexico time and time again. It is a very beautiful country of high mountains, green valleys, deserts, rivers, and lakes. In addition to scenery, however, Mexico is also rich in the archeological remains of its great past. Much of the Aztec archeology has been gathered into the Museum of History and Anthropology in Mexico City. Other remains can be seen in ruins in and around Mexico City, Cholula, and Oaxaca.

The craftsmanship achieved by the people during Aztec times still lives in the people of Mexico today. The market of Mexico City itself, as well as those in any of its big cities, such as Toluca, Puebla, and Oaxaca, are filled with the handicrafts of the Indians. There are beautiful baskets and mats, outstanding wood carvings, pottery of all shapes, colors, and designs. There is clay sculpture, stonework, tinware, ironware. There are outstanding hand-loomed fabrics, laces, and tooled leather. There is gold and silver jewelry, designed by gifted Mexican silversmiths.

Despite the centuries of living under foreign rule and the poverty the Mexicans endured, they have kept their sense of beauty and design and their pride in crafts. Some say that the only handicraft today with a style of its own is that of Mexico. The Aztecan Indians have kept their identity and quiet pride.

In many respects the life in present-day Aztecan villages is not very different from the life in the Aztec Empire. The homes are still crowded together in a village some distance from the outlying fields. These are still one-room houses with simple fireplaces for cooking indoors and for warmth in cool weather. Some have one or two tiny windows, others only a door. An outdoor lean-to is used for cooking in summer. The homes are of stone, covered with mud plaster and

THE UNITED STATES OF MEXICO

chinked with mud. In the southern part of
Mexico they are built of wattle and adobe brick.
The roofs used to be of thatch. Later wood shin-
gles were used. But today, because wood is getting
so scarce, the people are encouraged to use tile for
their roofs. A farmer nowadays still owns his
home.

The inside of the home is furnished as simply
as the farmers' huts in Aztecan times. There is
usually a bed for the parents, but the children
sleep on the floor. The baby sleeps near its mother
for the first few years. Later he will join his
brothers and sisters on the mats on the floor.

There may be two or three low chairs in the
home for adults to sit on. The children sit on the
floor. And the parents, too, find sitting on a mat
more comfortable and less confining. The mother
works in a sitting position on the floor close to the
fireplace and to her comal, or griddle. When in
use, her cooking utensils are placed around the
fire. Otherwise, they are hung neatly on the wall
over it. Today, as in Aztecan times, the tortilla is
still the main food. Bread is eaten, but it is not
usually baked at home. It is bought in the small

village store. For this, cash is necessary, since the Aztec of today no longer exchange goods in trade but use Mexican money. The cash income in these villages is very low. Therefore, bread is only eaten on special occasions. As in the old days, the corn the farmer grows is still stored by the family in the home or in a separate little building. They try to make it last from harvest to harvest.

A woman still soaks the shelled corn overnight and then crushes it on her metate. There is a metate on the floor in each household, and a woman or her daughter kneels behind it, grinding the corn for the next meal. Nowadays there are also stores in the villages where corn dough for tortillas can be purchased. Some families use small meat grinders to grind the soaked corn. The people still eat two meals a day, one early in the morning before they go off to work in the fields, and the second when they return home. Besides the metate, each household has a few stone grinders to grind the chili that goes into the sauce for the tortillas or into the cooked beans, the frijoles.

There are small stores in each village where a woman buys certain necessities for the household, such as salt, sugar, coffee, and chocolate. There is also a butcher shop, where on certain days of the week a red flag announces that a sheep or pig or cow has been slaughtered. The women then buy fresh meat if they can afford it.

The households are still quite self-sufficient, as they were in the old days. Each village woman now raises her own chickens and pigs, as well as turkeys. She has a little garden near her home for the herbs and peppers she needs for flavoring. Fruit trees have been planted by the men, and the women dry the fruit, so it will keep until the next fall. In the fall, after harvest, the little homes are garlanded with strings of drying peppers and sliced fruits. Women go out into the fields, as they used to in the old days, to gather wild greens. The man of the house and the boys are mainly responsible for bringing in wood for the fire. Charcoal is now being made in the villages. It is more convenient and quicker than wood chips or wood.

The dogs the Spanish introduced have spread all over Mexico. A dog is a guardian of the home and a hunter and companion. They are not eaten any more. The donkey, or burro, which the Spanish introduced, has become indispensable, since it is easy to feed, is a good beast of burden, and can be mounted when going back and forth over long distances. The Mexicans, however, still walk a great deal.

The Spanish also introduced the large, shady straw hat, the sombrero. Although the nobility wore all sorts of headdresses, the common people usually went about bareheaded. Now the sombrero is worn universally, in all shapes and forms. Some are very large, heavy, and expensive. A man buys one of these sombreros for a lifetime. These straw hats are being made today in villages where palms grow nearby.

The clothing of the men changed to white homespun trousers and a loose, long-sleeved shirt. For cool weather, the mantles are now slit in the center, so they will slip on over the head, thus keeping both the chest and back warm. They have kept their Nahuatl name of *tzalape*, or, as they say it in Mexico today, zarape (sah-rah'-pay). In cold weather the sides are tied together for warmth. Actually, the zarape has many advantages over the fitted overcoat, since it allows greater freedom of movement in working and walking and keeps hands and knees warm. At night the zarape becomes an additional blanket. Sandals are still the main footwear, but the leather sole is often replaced with heavy rubber from used auto tires.

The farmers work daily in the fields. They plant corn, beans, peppers, squash, and cotton, as in the old days, and also wheat and sugar cane. The ground is plowed today by teams of oxen— also brought in by the Spanish. In some villages, if the farmers can afford it, they pool their funds and get a tractor. But the hoeing is still done by hand. Each corn plant gets hoed about three times during its growing period.

Land is now bought and sold. To own land is the most desirable kind of wealth for these Indians. The farmers who cannot afford to own their land rent it instead.

The livelihood of the farmer depends on his harvest, plus any other skills or crafts he has to supplement it for a cash income, which can be used for other foods, medicines, extras in clothing and shoes, and for contributions to the church. The men today are the skilled weavers of Mexico, and the weaving done is of the finest type.

The villages are self-governing, as they were in Aztecan times. The council is elected by the men of the village. The council then selects one of its members to be the mayor. The mayor's responsibility is to preserve law and order and to care for the schools and the irrigation canals. He also acts as judge. Through its mayor, the village council asks the federal authorities for the things they need, such as aid to their local school and better roads. The council also elects a treasurer for a three-year term, a secretary, and a collector. The secretary has to keep the village records of births, marriages, deaths, land and home ownership, and taxes paid to the federal government. The collector watches over the taxes.

These Indians are poor by our standards. But by their own standards, they have enough to make a living. They have their small homes, their daily work, and their families. Relatives and neighbors will always help them. Above all, they have their religion. Their poverty is not that of the totally uprooted people in the big towns.

Some Indians in the cities do manage to make a living, but many of the others who have drifted away from their villages have sunk into stark, hopeless poverty. They live in broken-down hovels on the outskirts of the cities. Unlike the people in the villages, these uprooted city dwellers have no friends or relatives nearby to give them a helping hand. They live from day to day. Many drink too much. Many are sick because of poor food and housing. They have no money to buy medicine. Some become criminals and are jailed. Few have the good sense to return to their old villages. But even these people are not without hope for the future.

Religion to the Mexican farmers is as important as it was in the days of the Aztec. After four centuries the Mexican descendants of the Aztec are still a very religious people. Most of their pleasures and joys continue to be associated with their religion.

We will never know how deep the shock must have been to the Aztec when they found their gods unwilling to help them in the most desperate time in their lives. Nor will we ever know the pain of a people who see their temples shattered. Immediately after the conquest, Spanish missionaries came to convert the Aztec to Christianity. The Spanish conquerors were Catholic, and the religion they taught the Indians was Catholicism.

Perhaps the hardest thing for the Aztec to understand was that the new god, Christ, *loved* the people. The Aztecan gods needed the people, but the people had no love for the gods. They were afraid of them and felt indebted to them. Living in subjection, the Indians gradually began to understand Christ's humility, His consideration for and love of the poor. They were poor now, and so they began to feel that Christ was watching over them, that they were now Christ's chosen people. He suffered for them, too.

They could understand the new religion only with their old beliefs. These included miracles, magic, and prophecy. The Aztecans even adapted their old calendar to the new feast days, such as the birth of Christ, the Resurrection, and the New Year. It must have been a great relief to know that no longer need they fear the fifty-two-year cycles that might end the world.

The Indians call Christ Totatzin in Nahuatl. This means *father* and may also mean *sun*. When men awaken at dawn and see the sun rise, they say, "Our Lord Totatzin is coming."

To these people, the saints are additional gods, who help Christ run the world. The saints take the place of the farmers' gods. They bring thunder and lightning, clouds and rain. Each village has a saint who looks after its people. They pray to their patron saint to ask God to bring rain when there is a drought. They pray to him for health when they are sick. They pray to him for a big harvest.

About ten years after the Spanish conquest, when the Christian teachings had begun to have some effect among the Indians, a poor man, who had been newly baptized and named Juan Diego, was on his way to church in a village not far from Mexico City. As he passed a hill, he believed he saw a vision. The Holy Virgin came down toward him and asked him to go at once to his bishop, Juan Zumarraga, and tell him to build a church on this spot. At first Bishop Zumarraga refused to believe the humble Indian. But the next day Juan Diego came to church once more and said that the Virgin had appeared to him again, saying, "Tell your bishop that it is the Virgin Mary, Mother of God, who sends thee." But Bishop Zumarraga still doubted the man.

As Juan Diego related, when the Virgin appeared to him for the third time, the poor man told her that he needed proof to convince his bishop. The apparition commanded him to go pluck some roses at the top of the hill. The day was December 12, and Juan Diego knew that no roses would grow there in winter. Nonetheless, he went up obediently. "There were roses in bloom on top of the hill," he later told his bishop. He picked them and gave them to the Virgin. She wrapped them in his zarape and ordered him to take them to the bishop.

Juan Diego came to the bishop with his bundle and opened it. But instead of roses, the zarape bore a painting of the Virgin of Guadalupe, a gentle-faced Indian maiden. As a result of this vision, a beautiful church was built on the hilltop

of Tepeyac and the image of the Virgin was placed above the altar, so it could be seen radiating rays of light.

This added another festive day to the Mexican calendar. In the minds of the Indians the Virgin of Guadalupe is Tonantzin, the mother of earth and corn. The waters of the spring near where she first appeared to Juan Diego are said to have miraculous healing powers. On December 12 thousands of pilgrims come to the Church of Our

Lady of Guadalupe to pray and to drink of the holy water.

The missionaries introduced another new custom when they asked the parents of an infant to get godparents for the baptism of their child. This new interrelationship among the villagers took root and grew into a system of friendly obligations and responsibility, making family and village ties even stronger.

The parents select an older couple in their village to accompany them to church for the baptismal ceremony. The godparents then pay the baptismal fee to the church and give a party in the child's honor. As the child grows, the parents come to the godparents for advice. The godparents visit the child regularly. As the child grows older, he helps his godparents with the household and in the field. When he begins to earn money, he always brings them gifts and treats them with the same respect he gives to his parents.

When a young man becomes engaged, his parents ask the godparents to act as marriage godparents. But if the godparents feel too old, they help select a different set of marriage godparents for the couple. The marriage godparents organize the engagement procession to carry gifts of fruit, candy, and cakes to the girl's parents. They also pay some of the wedding expenses.

As in the days of the Tenochca, the girl's parent are "losing" a daughter, and so gifts are brought to them to make the loss bearable. The two sets of godparents, parents, grandparents, and other relatives usually accompany the bridegroom to the girl's home. The young couple also exchange simple gifts—a handkerchief, a shawl, a photograph, earrings, ribbons. Everyone in the village watches the procession. The engagement party stops at each street corner to dance to the music of the band, which the bridegroom's family hires. At the engagement feast the couple announce their wedding day, which is usually on a Sunday among these farming people. Before the wedding they appear before the village secretary to record the marriage. Later at the church the priest reads the banns, and he, too, announces on what Sunday the marriage will take place.

On the Saturday before the wedding the

couple visit both sets of parents to receive their blessings. But they spend the night at the home of their marriage godparents. In the morning the godfather helps the groom dress. The godmother helps the girl dress and braids her hair. Many young women still wear their hair in two long braids, as in the Aztecan times.

The marriage ceremony is simple. The couple meet in church. The marriage godmother gives the priest two rings, which he places on their fingers, and as they join hands, he pronounces them man and wife. Everyone is invited to go to the marriage godparents' home for a wedding feast.

In a village everyone is thus tied to everyone else by being somebody's godparent. People even select godparents for the purchase of a cow or a truck, for housewarmings, and when opening a store. They believe that godparents bring them luck. As of old, a man has to work for the village welfare and for its church, to gain respect and a position in the village council. Godparents respect one another and try to help one another. They refer to each other with respect as *com-*

padre (kom-pah'-dray), which means friend. No one hesitates to ask his *compadre* for favors.

The villagers love gatherings and festivals, or fiestas, as they say in Mexico. The village council usually supports a fiesta and everyone helps to make it a success. A fiesta starts as a religious ceremony and ends up as a noisy social gathering, enjoyed by everyone.

If the village does not have a band of its own, they invite a band from another village and pay its members out of the village treasury. The band is usually a drum and a few wind instruments. People greet the band as it comes off the bus and hang garlands of flowers on the musicians. The procession starts at the village plaza. Some people carry candles. Women and children carry flowers. In the plaza vendors set up little booths, shaded with white squares of homespun cloth, for lemonade, orange juice, apple juice, and soft drinks. Women with baskets on their heads sell fresh tortillas, which people buy and dip in a chili sauce, adding a spoonful of frijoles. In large earthen pots they boil stews and corn in its husks. They sell sweets, goat cheese, and other cheeses.

The procession wanders through the village streets, gaining more and more followers. It finally ends up at the church, which the men have decorated with fresh greens and flowers. Everyone places his candle at the altar. On the steps of the church, small dishes of copal incense are also lit up—a carry-over from ancient times. Before the services begin, priests come out in their embroidered vestments covered with lace, and the people kneel in silent prayer. Outside, a team of men, assigned to the job, shoot off several firecrackers. Then everyone gives thanks for being alive and well. The saints will be pleased and honored with the ceremony and will bring only good to the people.

People still believe in magic and witchcraft. In each village there is a witch or two. When it is suspected that some evil is being brought on by these witches, the people refer to them as bad witches. At other times, when illness strikes, the people turn to them for help. Then they call them "wise ones" and "curers" and readily accept the chants the witches use to drive out illness. Many of the herbs used by them have come down from ancient times, and some are effective. However, when people fall ill they use modern medicines along with herbs, snakeskins, and charms. Illness, like good health, is entirely in the hands of God, Whose mysterious ways the modern Indians cannot probe any more than their ancestors could. They, therefore, accept life and death with equal dignity, as becomes God's chosen people.

INDEX

* Indicates illustrations